Postpartum Disorders

THE STATE OF
MENTAL ILLNESS
AND ITS THERAPY

THE STATE OF MENTAL ILLNESS AND ITS THERAPY

Postpartum Disorders

Autumn Libal

Mason Crest

Mason Crest
450 Parkway Drive, Suite D
Broomall, PA 19008
www.masoncrest.com

Printed in the Hashemite Kingdom of Jordan.

First printing
9 8 7 6 5 4 3 2 1

Series ISBN: 978-1-4222-2819-7
ISBN: 978-1-4222-2832-6
ebook ISBN: 978-1-4222-8993-8

The Library of Congress has cataloged the
    hardcopy format(s) as follows:

        Library of Congress Cataloging-in-Publication Data

Libal, Autumn.
  [Drug therapy and postpartum disorders]
  Postpartum disorders / Autumn Libal.
     pages cm. – (The state of mental illness and its therapy)
  Audience: Age 12.
  Audience: Grade 7 to 8.
  Revision of: Drug therapy and postpartum disorders. 2004.
  Includes bibliographical references and index.
  ISBN 978-1-4222-2832-6 (hardcover) – ISBN 978-1-4222-2819-7 (series) – ISBN 978-1-4222-8993-8 (ebook)
  1. Postpartum psychiatric disorders–Juvenile literature. 2. Postpartum psychiatric disorders–Treatment–Juvenile literature. 3. Postpartum psychiatric disorders–Chemotherapy–Juvenile literature. I. Title.
  RG850.L53 2014
  618.7'6061–dc23
                              2013008259

Produced by Vestal Creative Services.

www.vestalcreative.com

CONTENTS

Introduction
by Mary Ann McDonnell

Teenagers have reason to be interested in psychiatric disorders and their treatment. Friends, family members, and even teens themselves may experience one of these disorders. Using scenarios adolescents will understand, this series explains various psychiatric disorders and the drugs that treat them.

Diagnosis and treatment of psychiatric disorders in children between six and eighteen years old are well studied and documented in the scientific journals. A paper appearing in the *Journal of the American Academy of Child and Adolescent Psychiatry* in 2010 estimated that 49.5 percent of all adolescents aged 13 to 18 were affected by at least one psychiatric disorder. Various other studies have reported similar findings. Needless to say, many children and adolescents are suffering from psychiatric disorders and are in need of treatment.

Many children have more than one psychiatric disorder, which complicates their diagnoses and treatment plans. Psychiatric disorders often occur together. For instance, a person with a sleep disorder may also be depressed; a teenager with attention-deficit/hyperactivity disorder (ADHD) may also have a substance-use disorder. In psychiatry, we call this comorbidity. Much research addressing this issue has led to improved diagnosis and treatment.

The most common child and adolescent psychiatric disorders are anxiety disorders, depressive disorders, and ADHD. Sleep disorders, sexual disorders, eating disorders, substance-abuse disorders, and psychotic disorders are also quite common. This series has volumes that address each of these disorders.

Major depressive disorders have been the most commonly diagnosed mood disorders for children and adolescents. Researchers don't agree as to how common mania and bipolar disorder are in children. Some experts believe that manic episodes in children and adolescents are underdiagnosed. Many times, a mood disturbance may occur with another psychiatric disorder. For instance, children with ADHD may also be depressed. ADHD is just one psychiatric disorder that is a major health concern for children, adolescents, and adults. Studies of ADHD have reported prevalence rates among children that range from two to 12 percent.

Failure to understand or seek treatment for psychiatric disorders puts children and young adults at risk of developing substance-use disorders. For example, recent research indicates that those with ADHD who were treated with medication were 85 percent less likely to develop a substance-use disorder. Results like these emphasize the importance of timely diagnosis and treatment.

Early diagnosis and treatment may prevent these children from developing further psychological problems. Books like those in this series provide important information, a vital first step toward increased awareness of psychological disorders; knowledge and understanding can shed light on even the most difficult subject. These books should never, however, be viewed as a substitute for professional consultation. Psychiatric testing and an evaluation by a licensed professional is recommended to determine the needs of the child or adolescent and to establish an appropriate treatment plan.

Foreword
by Donald Esherick

We live in a society filled with technology—from computers surfing the Internet to automobiles operating on gas and batteries. In the midst of this advanced society, diseases, illnesses, and medical conditions are treated and often cured with the administration of drugs, many of which were unknown thirty years ago. In the United States, we are fortunate to have an agency, the Food and Drug Administration (FDA), which monitors the development of new drugs and then determines whether the new drugs are safe and effective for use in human beings.

When a new drug is developed, a pharmaceutical company usually intends that drug to treat a single disease or family of diseases. The FDA reviews the company's research to determine if the drug is safe for use in the population at large and if it effectively treats the targeted illnesses. When the FDA finds that the drug is safe and effective, it approves the drug for treating that specific disease or condition. This is called the labeled indication.

During the routine use of the drug, the pharmaceutical company and physicians often observe that a drug treats other medical conditions besides what is indicated in the labeling. While the labeling will not include the treatment of the particular condition, a physician can still prescribe the drug to a patient with this disease. This is known as an unlabeled or off-label indication. This series contains information about both the labeled and off-label indications of psychiatric drugs.

I have reviewed the books in this series from the perspective of the pharmaceutical industry and the FDA, specifically focusing on the labeled indications, uses, and known side effects of these drugs. Further information can be found on the FDA's website (www.FDA.gov).

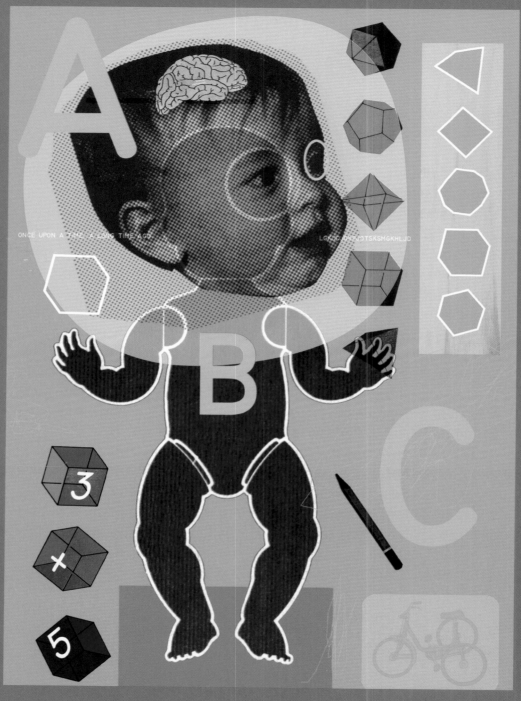

Becoming a mother is often discussed as one of life's most joyful experiences. For many women, however, the time directly after childbirth is filled with confusion, exhaustion, and loneliness.

Chapter One

What Are Postpartum Disorders?

The baby was crying—again. This was the fourth time tonight. Sandra squinted through the dark at the clock's glowing red numbers. It was three in the morning, and she just couldn't drag herself from bed one more time. She put her hands over her ears, trying to block out the plaintive cries of her daughter who was imprisoned in a crib across the hall.

No matter how loudly her daughter cried, her wails could not penetrate the veil of Sandra's melancholy. Three weeks after the birth of her first child, Sandra felt like she was drowning in a dark ocean of motherhood. This was not the way it was supposed to be; everyone told her that she would be happy. Her friends and family had described in joyous detail the overwhelming feeling of love and purpose that would envelop her at her daughter's birth. No one had prepared Sandra for the heavy fog of dread and loss that descended upon her. Even when the nurse had handed her the crying, bruised, purple and pink bundle in the delivery room, Sandra had fought the urge to hand back the bundle and run.

Sandra tried discussing her feelings with her mother. Her mother simply waved her hand, gave a condescending smile, and said, "It's just the baby blues. You'll snap out of it in a few days," and went back to crooning over her new granddaughter. But Sandra wasn't

Society tells us that babies are "bundles of joy." Having grown up with this belief, many women are dismayed if their bundles of joy don't bring the immediate happiness they expected.

snapping out of it, and she was relying on her mother more and more for the baby's care. Some days, Sandra could hardly leave her room at all. Her mother began scolding her, telling her how important it was for her to bond with her daughter in these early days. Sandra didn't want to bond. She wanted to turn the clock back nine months before any of this had happened. When she did spend time with her daughter, she found herself whispering, "I hate you. I wish you had never been born."

When Sandra heard these words coming out of her mouth she hated herself. She knew that somewhere inside of her she loved her daughter and was deeply grateful the baby had come into the world. And yet those feelings were locked away in some dark chamber buried deep beneath a mountain of sadness. Sandra could not find the energy to move this enormous mountain out of her way, and she feared she would never reach the love, joy, and happiness she wanted for her daughter and for herself. She had been so happy before her daughter was born—so why couldn't she find the energy to be the mother her daughter deserved?

Discussion

According to the traditionally held beliefs of our society, the early days of motherhood are supposed to be a time of happiness, excitement, love, and bonding between mother and child. For many women, however, the reality of motherhood is very different from this rosy ideal. Many new mothers find the adjustment from independent, pre-baby life to the constant demands of new parenthood to be difficult, exhausting, lonely, and even depressing. Though there are women who quickly find happiness and fulfillment in their new role as mothers, there are also many women who during this time are surprised to discover that the reality of motherhood is not as immediately joyful and satisfying as they had expected.

The time directly after giving birth to a child is filled with physical, emotional, and social changes. Many of these changes that occur puerperium and postpartum can make a woman vulnerable to

When a child is born, the mother's body experiences a dramatic hormonal shift as it adjusts from pregnancy to preparing to breastfeed the newborn.

sadness and depression. The word "puerperium" refers to the time directly after birth when the mother's body is physically recovering from the effects of pregnancy and delivery. This physical recovery period usually lasts about six weeks. The word "postpartum" refers to all the changes—physical, emotional, mental, and social—that occur in the mother's life during the first year after giving birth.

Postpartum Blues

The early puerperium period involves many drastic physical changes that can affect a new mother's mood and sense of emotional and physical well-being. As soon as a child is born, hormone levels in

Hormones are the powerful chemical messengers of your body. For example, imagine that you're just about to play in the championship game. Your hands are sweaty, your heart is pounding, and your knees are shaking. These feelings are caused in part by a surge of the hormone adrenaline. In nature, adrenaline is part of the "fight or flight" response. When animals are in danger, adrenaline gives them extra strength, courage, and energy to fight their attacker or make a quick getaway. When you're under stress, adrenaline causes similar physical and emotional responses in your body. Another example of the power of hormones involves women's menstruation. Once each month, special hormones tell a woman's body to release an egg and prepare for possible pregnancy. These hormones can also trigger something known as premenstrual syndrome or PMS. PMS can involve feelings such as sadness, frustration, and irritability. Some people don't understand PMS and think that it's not real, or that it's just an excuse for "irrational" emotions. None of this is true. Emotions triggered by hormones are just as real as any other emotions. You should always pay attention to your body and respect the way you feel—even when your feelings are related to hormones.

the mother's body go through a dramatic shift as her body adjusts from growing a child inside her to preparing to breastfeed and care for the newborn. Many women develop depressive symptoms such as crying, irritability, and fatigue around three to five days after giving birth. This is also the period of time when a new mother begins lactating, and some doctors believe these emotional symptoms are related to the hormones that are responsible for causing lactation.

lactating: Producing milk and capable of nursing.

This temporary period of sadness after the birth of a child has been given many names, including the "baby blues," "postpartum blues," "third-day blues," "fourth-day blues," and "tenth-day blues." Some studies estimate that as many as 70 to 80 percent of new mothers experience the temporary postpartum blues. Fortunately, this common experience is usually not severe enough to adversely affect the mother's relationship with the child and will end within the first two weeks after giving birth.

Though the biological changes that occur in a woman's body after giving birth can have a powerful effect on her emotional condition, other factors influence new mothers as well. Oftentimes a new mother may experience disappointment and confusion during the postpartum period as she is adjusting to her new social role. After having children, parents must come to terms with a change in their personal identities. They are no longer the independent individuals they once were. They must adjust to losing the autonomy they had enjoyed and accept their new responsibilities as parents. Today, most North American women work outside the home. A woman who is accustomed to working and building a career, for example, may suddenly feel restless and isolated as she is thrown from the atmosphere of the office into caring for a newborn at home. She may long for the mental stimulation, adult conversation, challenges, and sense of accomplishment that her work gave her. New mothers often face confusion as they struggle with their changing sense of self, asking, "Who am I without my work?" or "Who am I now that I have a child?"

autonomy: A condition of independence in which one can make decisions and act on one's own authority.

As their lives shift to revolve around caring for a child, new parents may also miss the time they formerly spent alone together or the fun they had socializing with friends. It is perfectly natural for both mothers and fathers to feel some confusion and sadness as they grieve the passing of their old way of life. However, this natural grieving usually gives way to acceptance and satisfaction with the new role of parenthood.

For 10 to 20 percent of new mothers, however, the negative feelings that can accompany early motherhood are something far more serious than postpartum blues or a simple adjustment period. Some women suffer from conditions known as postpartum disorders. Currently, the majority of the medical field recognizes two types of postpartum disorders: postpartum depression and postpartum psychosis.

Postpartum Depression

The term "postpartum depression" is used to refer to major depression whose onset begins shortly after the birth of a child and appears to be directly linked either psychologically or biologically to the new role that goes along with caring for an infant. Characteristics of depression include symptoms relating to one's mental state or emotions, such as overwhelming sadness, anxiety, confusion, and irritability, as well as physical symptoms such as fatigue, headaches, loss of appetite, and insomnia. The symptoms of postpartum depression can begin any time within the first six months after giving birth and last for more than two weeks.

In addition to the general symptoms of major depression, women with postpartum depression often have additional symptoms relating to the baby. These may include excessive anxiety about the baby's health and safety, feelings of inadequacy as a mother, and even negative feelings toward the baby or thoughts of harming the child. Physical abuse caused by a mother's postpartum depression is very rare, but a caring physician needs to evaluate the situation for the possibility of abuse.

psychologically: Relating to or caused by the mind or emotions.

biologically: Relating to or caused by the physical body.

Although very few mothers with postpartum depression act on their thoughts of harming their children, postpartum depression can involve serious risks to babies in other ways. Whereas the less serious postpartum blues do not interfere with the woman's ability to mother her child, the more serious postpartum disorder of postpartum depression does adversely affect the mother–child relationship. For example, the new mother may feel too depressed to take interest in her baby or adequately care for the child. In the above story, we see that Sandra's depression keeps her from responding to her daughter's cries. Furthermore, Sandra is relying on her mother to take care of the child. The first year of life is a vital period for a child's physical, mental, and emotional development. Child neglect or damage to the parent–child relationship that occurs within the first year of life can have long-term consequences for the child's physical, mental, and emotional growth.

On the other hand, postpartum depression can cause a new mother such excessive anxiety about the child's well-being and safety that she cannot function normally. Obsessive worrying about the child's safety can lead to loss of sleep, increased tension, an unwillingness to accept help from others, and damage to personal relationships. The exhaustion, fears, and feelings of inadequacy as a parent that result from the excessive anxiety of postpartum depression can make it difficult or even impossible for a mother to interact with her baby in a normal, healthy, and ultimately beneficial way.

There is no way to determine who will develop postpartum depression and who will not, but certain risk factors exist. Experts have conflicting views as to whether depression during pregnancy is an indication of whether or not a woman will experience postpartum depression after birth. Many women become depressed during the physical and emotional upheaval of pregnancy, and some scientists say that experiencing depression at this time does not affect whether or not a woman will experience depression after her child is born. Other scientists, however, say that a woman who has depression during pregnancy may in fact be more likely to continue experiencing depression once her child is born.

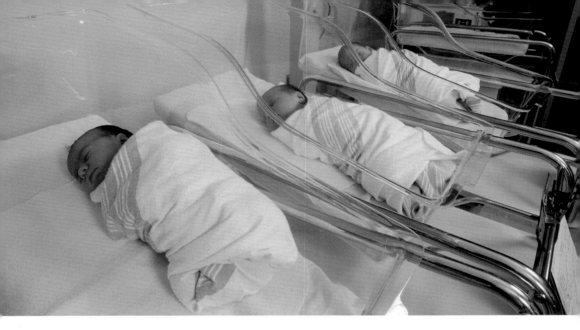

These newborns are in their first few days of life. In the past, babies were often whisked away from their mothers as soon as they were born, but the first hours after birth are a vital period for creating strong bonds between mother and child.

Biological influences may make certain women more susceptible to developing postpartum depression. Women with a history of clinical depression or severe depression in the premenstrual period may be more likely to suffer from postpartum depression. However, biology may not be the most important factor in whether or not a woman will experience postpartum depression.

clinical depression: A depressive state that is long lasting and serious enough to interfere with the tasks of everyday life.

Although the temporary postpartum blues may be related to a new mother's fluctuating hormone levels, no conclusive data suggests that the longer term condition of postpartum depression is directly caused by hormonal imbalance. Instead, postpartum depression may be strongly influenced

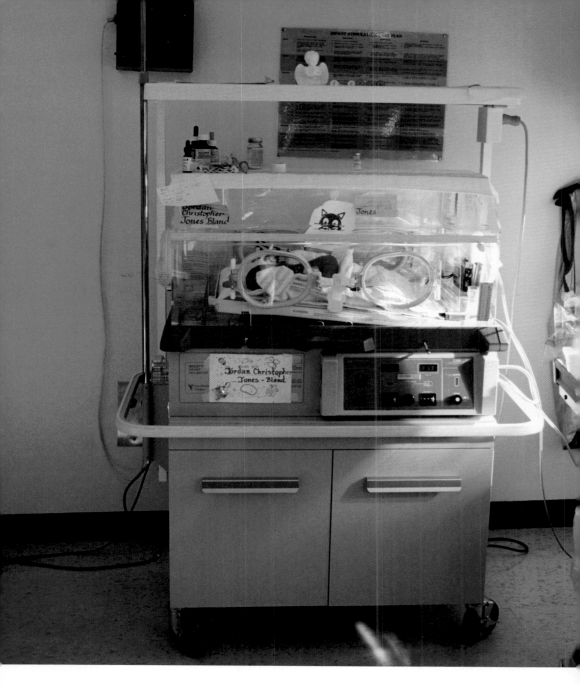

Babies born prematurely face many medical challenges. Mothers who give birth to premature babies also appear to be at greater risk for developing postpartum disorders.

by external factors such as social and environmental conditions. For example, studies have shown that women who lack spousal or familial support, are having difficulties in their marital relationships, or do not have a partner to help care for the new child have a higher incidence of developing postpartum depression. Women who have strong social support networks (such as support groups for new mothers, close family members, or a spouse or partner who helps with the child) have a lower incidence of developing postpartum depression. Women who suddenly stop working to care for a new child may also be at higher risk for developing postpartum depression. Traditional societies in which women have large, extended families and new mothers participate in community and ritual activities have lower rates of postpartum depression than does North American society.

None of these examples, however, proves that biological influences on the woman's body play no part in the development of postpartum depression. What is most likely is that postpartum depression is the result of a complicated mix of biological and social factors. Many scientists believe that biological factors, such as hormone fluctuation during and after pregnancy, make a woman vulnerable to depression, while social factors, such as familial support and marital conditions, determine whether the woman's vulnerability will develop into depression.

In addition to hormone levels and social support networks, other factors may also increase the likelihood of a new mother developing postpartum depression. Premature birth and the birth of twins both appear to be risk factors. This may be because the births and postpartum periods of preterm infants and twins are often accompanied by more physical and emotional stress than are the births of single, full-term infants. Women who suffer miscarriages or stillbirths appear to be at an increased risk for developing postpartum depression as well. Girls who have children while they are still in their adolescence

stillbirths: Births in which the child is delivered dead.

may also be at increased risk for developing depression after giving birth. In North America, women are often released from hospitals within forty-eight hours of giving birth, and this quick release from the hospital may leave new mothers frightened and unprepared for the challenges of caring for a newborn—and more vulnerable to developing postpartum depression.

Postpartum depression usually subsides within the first year after giving birth. However, mothers who develop postpartum depression are at an increased risk for experiencing recurrent depression throughout their lives. Furthermore, 20 to 30 percent of women

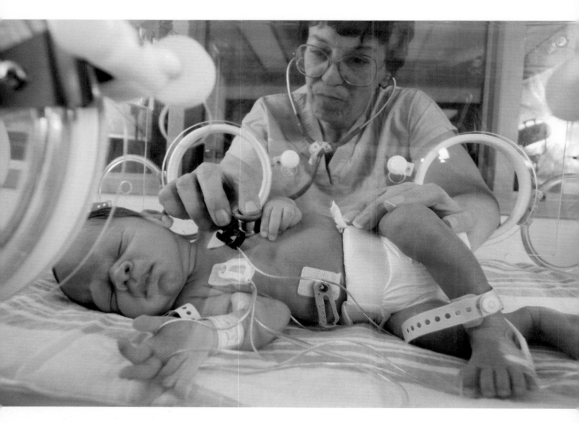

Having a child with a serious medical condition can be emotionally devastating for parents and can increase the risk of a woman developing postpartum depression.

Having a small life dependent on you can be a source of great joy and fulfillment—but it can also be an overwhelming responsibility when a woman is experiencing postpartum depression.

who experience postpartum depression after the birth of their first child will experience the disorder again if they have other children.

Postpartum Psychosis

The other type of postpartum disorder is a far more rare condition known as postpartum psychosis. Unlike postpartum depression, which 10 to 20 percent of all new mothers experience, postpartum psychosis only occurs in one to two out of every one thousand births. Also unlike postpartum depression in which external factors seem to play a large part in the condition's development, postpartum psychosis does appear to be largely biologically predetermined.

Your genes carry all the information you inherit from your parents; genes determine many of the ways you will grow and develop. Specific characteristics like your height and eye color were determined the moment the information in the sperm and egg combined to make your genes. Modern medicine has discovered that our genes also determine whether or not we develop some diseases such as Alzheimer's. A person who does not have the gene for Alzheimer's will not develop the disease. However, just because you have a gene for a certain condition does not necessarily mean you will develop that condition. Sometimes a person may be genetically predisposed toward a condition, but environmental factors will ultimately decide whether or not the person actually develops the condition.

schizophrenia: A mental disorder characterized by delusions, hallucinations, and disorganized thought processes.

predisposition: A tendency, inclination, or susceptibility.

cesarean section: A surgical procedure to deliver a baby.

One of the most important risk factors for developing postpartum psychosis is a family history of psychosis. Some psychotic disorders, such as schizophrenia, appear to be at least in part genetically predetermined. The reason some women develop psychotic disorders soon after pregnancy may be that these women already had a genetic predisposition to the disease, and the extreme physical stress of pregnancy and childbirth triggers the genetic condition. However, despite evidence that postpartum psychotic disorders are based on biology and genetics, social factors such as the absence of a partner to assist with childcare, miscarriage, stillbirth, and cesarean section may be risk factors as well.

A strand of DNA carries all the genetic information that makes each person unique.

Mothers are not the only ones who must adjust to the birth of a new child—fathers also have emotional adjustments to make.

Women who develop postpartum psychosis experience symptoms such as mania, delusions, and hallucinations beginning within the first three weeks after giving birth. The children of women experiencing postpartum psychosis may be in more immediate physical danger than the children of women experiencing postpartum depression. People experiencing delusions may not have awareness of what they are doing and may lack control over their actions. The delusions and unclear thinking of postpartum psychosis make the patient more likely to act on thoughts of harming her children. However, if postpartum psychosis is treated quickly and properly, children do not appear to be at any increased long-term risk.

One out of seven women who experience postpartum psychosis after the birth of their first child will experience the condition again if she has additional children.

mania: A state of abnormally intense activity that may be accompanied by extreme personality changes, violence, quickly alternating moods, or a dramatic sense of happiness.

delusions: Erroneous beliefs that are held despite all evidence to the contrary.

hallucinations: Seeing, hearing, or believing in objects or events that are not really there or have not occurred.

Men and Postpartum Disorders

When Robert first learned of his wife's pregnancy, he felt confused and disappointed. It was not that he didn't want children—he and Diane had been discussing their future family practically from the day they had met. He just hadn't expected this family to begin so soon. They were still filled with the excitement of early marriage; they had just returned from their honeymoon, were moving into a new house, and still had fun with their single friends. The idea of suddenly adjusting everything to accommodate a baby made Robert a little sad.

Fathers do not only experience emotional and social reactions to the birth of their children, they can have physical reactions as well. An example of how much a mother's pregnancy and childbirth can physically affect a father can be seen in something known as "sympathetic labor pains." When a child is born, the child's mother experiences pain in labor. Sometimes, however, the father also experiences sharp abdominal pain while the child is being born. These pains, for which there is no physical cause, are thought to be caused by the father's psychological identification with and desire to participate in the birth process. It is also relatively common for fathers to experience, as Robert did, a type of "sympathetic morning sickness" when the mother is pregnant.

Within a few days of learning that his wife was pregnant, however, Robert's initial disappointment began to subside and a new feeling took hold inside of him. "Father." The word echoed around his head like church bells. He was going to be a father! Pride swelled in him, nourishing him as if it were food or water. Robert knew he would make a great dad, and he couldn't wait to begin making preparations for his baby's arrival. He began converting the office of their new house into a nursery. Within three weeks of the time Diane found out she was pregnant, Robert was already painting walls and drawing up plans for a hand-built crib.

As Diane's pregnancy progressed, new changes came, and not all of them were as pleasant as Robert's new sense of purpose and pride. The nursery was taking shape as a sunny, colorful room, but Diane's mood was darkening and her energy was sapped. As Diane succumbed to violent bouts of morning sickness, Robert also began feeling weak and nauseous. He was always trying to soothe and help Diane, but sometimes as she was running sick to the bathroom, Robert would find himself heading in the direction to the other bathroom down the hall. Everyone took Diane's sickness very seriously,

New fathers may experience emotional, social, and even physical reactions after their babies' births.

Ideally, mothers and fathers should be equally involved in bonding with a new child.

offering advice on home remedies and tales of how they, too, had made it through the difficult months. But no one offered advice or even acknowledged Robert's physical reactions. At best, Diane's female friends treated Robert as if his sickness was sweet or charming; they would joke with Diane about how wonderful it must be to have such a sensitive husband who understood what she was going through. Robert didn't feel like his sensitivity was a good thing. He felt weak and incompetent.

Worse than his physical reaction to Diane's progressing pregnancy were the thoughts that began to descend upon him when Diane could feel the baby's movement inside her body. When these first movements began, Robert had been overwhelmed with emotion and couldn't wait to feel his baby's movements too. Diane would guide Robert's hand across her swelling stomach, but he couldn't feel a thing. Now it was five months into her pregnancy, and he still couldn't feel his child moving beneath Diane's skin. She tried to comfort him, saying it wouldn't be long before he could feel it too, but her attempts to make him feel better only made Robert feel sadder. He was becoming jealous of his wife. A great miracle was happening inside her, and he felt helpless to do anything but stand aside and watch. She was already feeling an intimate closeness with their child, but he only knew their child as his wife's distended belly. Robert felt like he was always a step behind, left out, almost as if he were being cheated because he was a man and couldn't participate in his baby's first nine months.

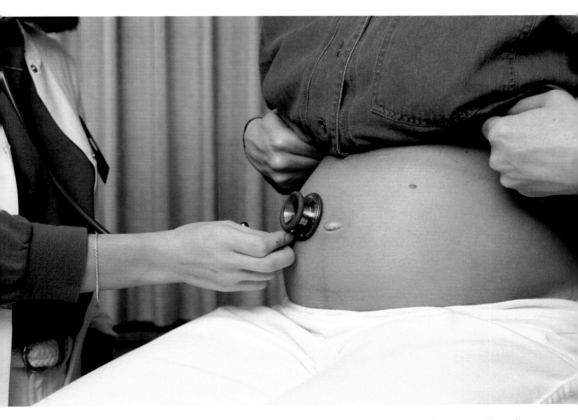

Since pregnancy revolves around the changes in the mother's body, some fathers feel left out.

Most fathers find parenthood as rewarding as mothers do, but sometimes life circumstances may complicate families.

Early parenthood is often a time of intense emotions for both parents.

Everyone's thoughts revolved around Diane and her swelling body. Robert grew to feel more and more like a bystander. Even Diane was beginning to withdraw. She spent a lot of time alone in the nursery that he had built, talking to her stomach instead of talking with him. She used to hug Robert as they fell asleep at night. Now her huge stomach was like a mountain between them. Most of the time she would roll over and lie with her back to Robert. If he tried to wrap his arms about her from behind, she groaned and said she was too uncomfortable, that she needed more space to stretch out. Robert's feelings of loneliness and exclusion grew. He thought it would help if he could tell someone what he was going through, but he felt too guilty. He felt selfish and more worthless than ever. No one would understand.

As the ninth month of Diane's pregnancy wore on, Robert longed for the baby to be born. He was sure the excitement of the new baby would change everything. He would be able to see, hold, and feed his child. He would no longer feel left out. But as Diane gave birth to their son, a part of Robert felt more sorrow than ever. Diane had given birth so quickly that by the time Robert had run back to grab her overnight bag from the car and found her hospital room, his son had already been born. Holding the newborn in his arms, he was filled with an indescribable joy, but part of him cried, "I missed it. I missed his birth, too."

Bringing his son home from the hospital was a joyous occasion. But in the following weeks, a quiet sense of despair clouded Robert's feelings toward fatherhood. His wife was on maternity leave, but every day Robert had to get up early and leave for work. He would glance wistfully at Diane still lying in bed. Then he would walk into the beautifully painted nursery and stand beside the crib he had built for his son. He watched the sleeping infant, trying to memorize the little face that was already growing and changing so quickly; then he would close the door and go to work. Every evening Robert returned home to hear the news of the day, how the baby had cried all morning, how his son had waved his arms at the sound of rock music, that Diane thought she'd seen his first smile. Each report made Robert wish that he were the one who could stay with the baby all day. Diane did not always give these reports happily. She was distraught and exhausted most of the time. But Robert couldn't muster the energy to understand her struggles for he was too deep in his own depression—once again his baby was growing and changing, and he was missing everything.

Discussion

Are the biological mothers of babies the only people who can develop postpartum depression? Some studies suggest not. In some cases, women who have adopted babies have experienced postpartum depression despite the fact they did not physically give birth to the new children. One study also showed that as many as

50 percent of partners of women with postpartum depression also developed clinically significant depression.

clinically significant: A condition severe enough to need medical intervention.

Just as the postpartum period involves many difficult physical, emotional, and social changes for a mother, it also poses similar challenges to the new father. Because men do not physically give birth to their children, their emotional difficulties in the early days of parenthood are not likely to be referred to as postpartum depression, but men can also face depression and psychiatric disorders following their children's births. Just as mothers must adjust to their new roles in parenthood, fathers also must come to terms with their own changing sense of self. This can be a difficult adjustment for any new parent.

In addition to adjusting to the role of parenthood, fathers sometimes feel displaced and left out since all the emphasis during pregnancy and welcoming the new child falls on the mother. Our society has a tendency to focus on the miracle of pregnancy, giving birth, and a mother's relationship with her child; fathers are sometimes forgotten. In Robert's case, feeling left out of the pregnancy, birth, and early childcare process led to true emotional distress. Just as society and the medical field must support new mothers, fathers' feelings must also be validated and their emotional needs addressed.

A century ago, North American women's lives were usually limited to childraising. These restrictions created emotional pressures.

Chapter Two

History of Therapy and Drug Treatment

f kept in this bed much longer, I will surely go mad. I suppose they believe I am mad already, and that is why I am here. Most days I sleep and eat and perhaps begin to feel quite better—until they bring the baby in to play. Then I feel suddenly overwhelmed and cry and wonder how I will ever be able to leave this room again.

I've been told I need rest, but it makes me itch and squirm with impatience. I've been told that my delicate nerves are causing this distress, but truly I believe it is the rest. I am so rested that I am ready to spring forth from this bed and run. I would run unrestrained and without direction. My only direction would be away, away from this bed, this room, and the baby who is now bawling to be fed.

Perhaps if I could run just a little I would feel better. Perhaps I would come back, in fact, to feed him and bathe him. But I would not suggest it. They fear I suffer from delusions as it is, without me saying I believe I have physical strength enough to walk from this bed.

Thank God I bore a son. I would not bring a girl into this world to suffer the same delicate female constitution. To be a woman, I have learned, is to have a disease. When you are with child, they lock you away like an illness that others must not see, as if you were in some frightful state. When your child is born, they confine you to bed like an invalid. And worst of all, if you do not seem demure, joyful, and grateful for their kindness, they say you are not well in the head, that your heart has been seized by some devilish sickness.

I have begun to agree. I am in fact diseased, and because of it I am not able to think or say or do anything but what I am directed. I suffer from the dreaded disease of being born a woman. Now I suppose there is no cure for my condition and the only treatment for me shall be to lie in this bed and rest as they say I should until there is nothing left of me but a breast for that baby to suckle.

Discussion

In the nineteenth century, the condition that we now call depression was referred to as "melancholia" and thought to mostly affect women. Doctors and society in general believed women were physically and mentally weaker than men and that this weakness made them prone to melancholia and other mental and physical ailments. At that time, most medical practitioners (all of whom were men) believed rest was the best thing for a woman suffering from melancholia. They believed the worst thing she could do for her health was to expose herself to stress—the stress of physical labor and the stress of intellectual activity. At this time in Western society, "thinking" was

Western: Relating to the countries and culture of Europe and America.

In the nineteenth and early twentieth centuries, many North Americans had a sentimental image of motherhood. Women were expected to create happy, rosy homes for their families— and they were not expected to have negative emotions. When they did, they were thought to be weak and in need of rest.

Throughout human history, women have often been seen as "weak"—both in the body and in the mind. Scientists of past centuries believed women were more susceptible to physical and mental illnesses than were men. In fact, many cultures throughout history saw mental illness as directly related to female biology, believing that conditions such as depression, mania, and hallucinations were caused by disease or malfunctioning of the female reproductive organs. In Greek civilization, for example, unexplained physical and psychological illness was called hysteria and was thought to occur only in women. ("Hysteria" comes from the Greek word for uterus.) The Greeks thought that the woman's uterus became dislodged from its normal location and would travel around the woman's body, causing pain or illness wherever it went. Four thousand years ago the Egyptians explained hysteria in the same way. In these cultures, what we now call postpartum depression would have been diagnosed as hysteria and different remedies would have been used to try to coax the uterus back to its proper location in the body.

feminists: People who advocate the rights and equality of women.

generally considered actually harmful to women.

Charlotte Perkins Gilman, a famous writer in the late nineteenth and early twentieth centuries and one of America's earliest feminists, did not agree with the social and medical opinions concerning women in her time. Gilman lived from 1860 to 1935, and in her life she wrote on subjects as varied as anthropology and ethics to fiction and satire, including the book *Women and Economics* and the short story, "Herland." Perhaps her most famous literary work, however, is a short story titled "The Yellow Wallpaper."

In earlier centuries, a woman who had just given birth would receive lots of physical and emotional support from other women.

"The Yellow Wallpaper" is the story of a woman who, suffering from what today might be called postpartum depression, is confined by her husband, a doctor, to a room in the country to rest. The woman's confinement is marked by frustration from the very beginning. She remarks of her husband, "You see, he does not believe I am sick! And what can one do? If a physician of high standing, and one's own husband, assures friends and relatives that there is really noth-

Charlotte Perkins Gilman

ing the matter with one but temporary nervous depression—a slight hysterical tendency—what is one to do?"

The woman goes on to lament, "So I take phosphates or phosphites—whichever it is—and tonics, and air and exercise, and journeys, and am absolutely forbidden to 'work' until I am well again. Personally, I disagree with their ideas. Personally, I believe that congenial work, with excitement and change, would do me good."

Unable to do anything other than rest as her husband has prescribed, the woman begins to hate the room in which she is confined and becomes obsessed with the yellow wallpaper covering her "prison." As the months drag by, she begins to see herself in the pattern of the wallpaper, for she comes to believe that the wallpaper's design shows a woman trapped behind bars from which she cannot escape. The woman eventually descends into madness and spends her final days of confinement stripping the paper from the walls of the room.

When "The Yellow Wallpaper" originally appeared in the January 1892 issue of *The New England Magazine*, it created a stir among readers and health care professionals. In fact, in the October 1913 issue of The Forerunner, Gilman reported that a doctor in Boston had said, "Such a story ought not to be written . . . it was enough to drive anyone mad to read it."

In that issue of The Forerunner, Gilman explained to her readers why she had written "The Yellow Wallpaper":

> For many years I suffered from a severe and continuous nervous breakdown tending to melancholia—and beyond. During about the third year of this trouble I went, in devout faith and some faint stir of hope, to a noted specialist in nervous diseases, the best known in the country. This wise man put me to bed and applied the rest cure, to which a still-good physique responded so promptly that he concluded there was nothing much the matter with me, and sent me home with solemn advice to "live as domestic a life as far as possible," to "have but two hours' intellectual life a day," and "never to touch pen, brush, or pencil again" as long as I lived. This was in 1887.

I went home and obeyed those directions for some three months, and came so near the borderline of utter mental ruin that I could see over.

Then, using the remnants of intelligence that remained, and helped by a wise friend, I cast the noted specialist's advice to the winds and went to work again—work, the normal life of every human being; work, in which is joy and growth and service, without which one is a pauper and a parasite—ultimately recovering some measure of power.

The circumstances that Gilman describes in "The Yellow Wallpaper" and in her own life are typical of how psychiatric illness in women was seen and treated in her day. Her stories and experiences also show how attitudes about women's place in society affect attitudes toward women's health and medical care.

Historically, many different factors have contributed to the recognition and treatment of postpartum disorders. For more than two thousand years, people have linked childbirth with mental health. Beliefs about the specific ways in which childbirth and the onset of psychological disorders are linked, however, have gone through drastic changes over the centuries.

In her book *Rock-a-by Baby: Feminism, Self-Help, and Postpartum Depression*, Verta Taylor discusses some of the ways that treatment for postpartum depression has changed throughout history and how these changes are related to larger issues and movements in society. She explains that throughout the nineteenth century, women's psychiatric illnesses were believed to be closely associated with pregnancy, childbirth, and other aspects of women's physiological makeup and functioning. However, this did not mean that women's physical and emotional complaints were always taken seriously. Women were often treated as if their physical and emotional symptoms were just a product of their weakness as women, as if being a woman was as much a disorder in itself as anything that might be ailing the woman. In such cases, women were often advised to rest, refrain from work, and limit "strenuous thinking."

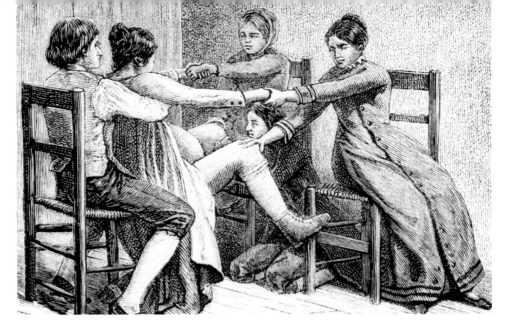

In the upper picture, a colonial woman gives birth with the help of a physician, his assistant, and two other women. In the seventeenth century, as shown in the lower picture, women who had just given birth lived in a secluded world, surrounded by other women. In both eras, women received social and emotional support from other women, but their conditions were not taken seriously by the medical world.

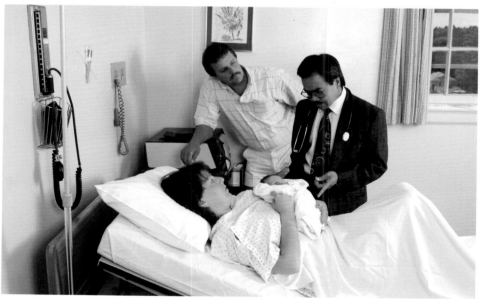

Women who give birth today have a very different experience than did women in the Middle Ages.

However, women experiencing post-partum depression and other psychiatric disorders were sometimes treated with drastic measures, such as being institutionalized in asylums and treated with extreme therapies such as electroshock.

Taylor points out that in the mid-twentieth century a change occurred in the way medicine and society viewed women's physical and psychiatric illnesses. At this time, feminism and the women's liberation movement created a backlash against beliefs associating women's medical problems with female physiological conditions and functions such as menstruation, pregnancy, and childbirth. This backlash was in large part due to the fact that men had historically used the sexes' biological differences as "proof" of women's inferiority and justification for social inequality. The women's movement sought to minimize emphasis on biological differences between men and women, and the effects of this movement can be seen in reactions in the medical field. For example, in 1952 the American Psychiatric Association dropped separate diagnostic categories of psychiatric illnesses related to childbirth from their *Diagnostic and Statistical Manual of Mental Disorders*. These diagnostic categories have never been replaced and are now contained in the larger diagnostic categories of major depression and psychosis.

However, the movement against emphasizing the biological differences between men and women apparently had an unexpected consequence. In the decades after the women's movement, many women once again felt that their physical and psychological symp-

institutionalized: To place a person into the care of an institution, such as a prison or a psychiatric hospital.

asylums: Places for the care of people requiring organized medical care or other supervision and assistance.

electroshock: The treatment of a mental disorder (especially depression) by transmitting electrical currents into parts of the brain.

In the 1980s and 1990s, a number of high-profile cases in the media contributed to raising the awareness of postpartum disorders, and society recognized a need for more social recognition and support for mothers. Cases in which deeply depressed or otherwise mentally ill mothers harmed or killed their infants made national headlines, triggering medical and social debate over the existence of postpartum disorders and increasing demand for accessible and reliable medical care for mothers.

toms were not taken seriously or adequately addressed by the medical field. Women suffering from postpartum disorders went undiagnosed and untreated, with sometimes devastating consequences.

Since the 1980s, North America has seen a resurgence of interest, research, and recognition of postpartum disorders. An important difference between the nineteenth century and the present day, however, is that in the past the male-dominated medical field often saw postpartum disorders as signs of women's weakness. The current push for recognition and treatment of postpartum disorders as significant medical issues is led by women demanding that the medical field take these conditions seriously.

New understanding of postpartum disorders has also led to new treatments. Thousands of years ago, treatments may have meant using herbs and salves to entice the uterus back to its proper location. Hundreds of years ago, women were told to rest and avoid intellectual pursuits immediately after childbirth. Now, treatment for postpartum disorders includes a combination of therapies meant to address the different physical, psychological, and social aspects that contribute to the development of these conditions. Talk therapy can address the confusion and emotional turmoil a woman

talk therapy: A treatment method that emphasizes talking rather than the use of drugs.

may feel after giving birth. Support groups often help women deal with the social isolation they may suddenly feel when becoming a new mom. Family counseling has been shown to be very beneficial in involving mothers' partners and other family members in caring for a new child and providing support to the new mother. Hormone replacement therapies can help women through the physical turbulence of the puerperium and postpartum periods.

Psychiatric drugs have also arisen as promising and important aspects of therapy. These drugs address the chemical imbalances that we now know play a part in many psychiatric illnesses and can help women experiencing postpartum depression. Psychiatric drugs have also been a valuable asset to treatment for postpartum psychosis.

Medical understanding of diseases and treatments change throughout history. Although modern medicine has made many advances in understanding physical and psychological aspects of postpartum disorders, even today's views of these and other disorders will continue to change. The opinions that modern medicine currently holds are constantly evolving, and as we learn more about the body and mind—and how they interact—our understanding of medical and psychiatric conditions and how to treat them will also evolve.

New mothers have to juggle many responsibilities and emotions.

Chapter Three

How Some Psychiatric Drugs Work

Bethany and Malcolm had only known each other for six months when they got married. Although they were in love and filled with hope and excitement for their future, they had never discussed marriage until they found out that Bethany was pregnant. They knew that they were young—Bethany was twenty-three and Malcolm was twenty-two—and that the pregnancy was unexpected, but they thought they would have a happy marriage and be good parents.

Malcolm's doubts began early in the marriage, but he did not share them with Bethany. He hadn't been prepared for how fast her body was going to change. He found something frightening about the way her stomach kept growing, expanding inch by inch, swelling so quickly that he swore it ballooned in the middle of the night.

Malcolm felt guilty about his thoughts toward Bethany's body. He knew he should be understanding, involved, and supportive, so he tried to hide his feelings. But the more he hid his thoughts from Bethany, the worse these thoughts became. He was having other troubling emotions as well. The further Bethany progressed in pregnancy, the more she depended on him to do things like make dinner, do the grocery shopping, and accompany her to the doctor. Malcolm's own parents had divorced when he was eight, and he had always resented all the ways that he had to help his mother in his father's absence. Now, he found himself experiencing the same feelings of resentment toward Bethany.

When Adam was born, Bethany found herself suddenly alone. She didn't know what had become of the easygoing, fun-loving guy she had married. Sure Malcolm and she still lived together, but she felt like she never saw him anymore. Her parents had agreed to help them financially while the baby was young, yet Malcolm had still insisted on taking a second job. He left early in the morning and got home after Bethany had already put Adam to bed. Bethany tried explaining how tired she was getting and how much she needed Malcolm's help, but her attempts always ended in frustrating and pointless arguments.

Bethany watched with resentment as Malcolm began going back to parties at his old college fraternity. Now he wasn't just gone while he was working; he made a point of being gone on the weekends as well. Bethany felt even more depressed when she realized that while Malcolm was out partying with all his old college friends, her friends were all gone. They had all moved away, or gotten jobs, or were at the parties Malcolm was at—but none of them seemed to care to visit her and the baby. She felt trapped at home and began to feel that the only thing in the world she had was Adam.

Bethany realized that in Malcolm's absence, if anything happened to Adam, no one would be around to help her. She worried constantly about filling the role of two parents, and she poured

Ideally, a baby should draw a couple closer together—but this isn't always the case.

Meeting a baby's needs can be overwhelming.

every ounce of energy she had into Adam—washing him, feeding him, holding him, and singing to him. She was afraid to leave him alone for a moment. When Malcolm was home, she didn't want to let him hold Adam for fear he would drop him. Though she was obsessive about Adam's care, she neglected caring for herself. Whole days would go by when she didn't eat and whole nights when she didn't sleep.

One night Malcolm came home late as usual to find Adam crying alone in his crib. Malcolm turned his back on Adam, called Bethany's name, and headed for the couch. As the TV blinked to life, he realized Adam had not stopped crying, and he called Bethany again—this time louder. Exasperated that she was not coming to take care of Adam's crying, Malcolm threw the remote control at the television and began stomping around the house calling for Bethany. He stopped abruptly in the bedroom doorway.

Bethany was lying motionless on the floor beside the bed. Malcolm ran to the bedside, knelt, and rolled her toward him. He shook her and called her name, but Bethany did not respond. Her skin felt clammy and her breathing came in quick, shallow puffs. Not knowing what else to do, Malcolm scooped her up and headed for the car. He was shocked by how light her body seemed, so different from the way it was during all those months of pregnancy. He had been so focused on the changes in her body then—how had he not noticed this sudden and frightening weight loss? With Bethany lying unconscious in the back seat, he raced for the hospital emergency room.

As Malcolm pulled up to the hospital, a new panic suddenly gripped him. Adam! He had left Adam home alone, crying in his crib! What if something happened to him while he was gone? How would Bethany ever forgive him? How would he forgive himself? Gripped with terror, Malcolm scooped Bethany from the back seat, rushed through the glass revolving door, and dumped her into the arms of a man in a white lab coat. Without explanation, he pushed back against the revolving door, leaving it spinning, and jumped into the car. As he flew toward home, Malcolm felt as though he was being torn in two. What kind of husband was he, dumping his wife into a stranger's arms and abandoning her without even knowing if she would be okay? What kind of father was he, rushing out of the house leaving his infant son behind—helpless and vulnerable?

In the days that followed, as Bethany recovered in the hospital from severe dehydration and exhaustion, Malcolm suddenly began to understand what Bethany had been going through at home. When the doctor first suggested to Malcolm that Bethany might have postpartum depression, Malcolm wondered how being home all day long could be anything other than relaxing and fun. Now home all day himself, Malcolm realized that caring for Adam was a full-time job—one that he did not feel equipped to handle. He knew that when Bethany returned, he wouldn't be able to abandon her the way he had before. He was going to have to learn to be a good husband and father—or none of them was going to make it very far.

In the weeks that followed, Malcolm and Bethany attended parenting classes and couples' counseling sessions together. Malcolm also went to individual therapy sessions in which he began to realize that taking a second job and spending more time with his college friends had been an attempt to run away not only from Bethany and Adam but also from his unresolved feelings about his family and childhood. Malcolm accepted that he needed to give up one of his jobs if he wanted to be a responsible spouse and parent, and he and Bethany accepted more financial help from her parents.

When Bethany saw all the changes Malcolm was making, she thought her own depression and anxiety would quickly disappear. But she was disappointed and frustrated to find that she was having a hard time overcoming her previous fears for Adam's well-being, and she still felt exhausted and irritable most of the time.

One month after her release from the hospital, Bethany was still feeling physically and emotionally overwhelmed. Because she was breastfeeding, Bethany had resisted her doctor's attempts to prescribe an antidepressant medication. Finally, however, Bethany realized that despite all the wonderful efforts and changes Malcolm had made, she still needed something more to help her through this difficult postpartum time. She found that within two weeks of beginning antidepressant medication, the cloud of anxiety and depression she had been living under began to clear. Eight months after their son's birth, Bethany and Malcolm felt like they were finally turning a corner and gaining control of their lives.

Discussion

In Bethany and Malcolm's story, we see that a variety of circumstances play into the depression and crisis that forms after their son's birth. They are both young and unprepared for becoming parents. They enter into the life changes of marriage and parenthood at the same time, doubling the stress they might otherwise feel in

A new baby is a demanding person!

Since children are emotionally and physically dependent on their parents, it is important for new mothers to seek the psychological and medical support they need.

just one of these situations. They are experiencing financial difficulties, which can place stress on a couple's relationship and be a precursor to developing depression. Malcolm has a family history that makes him emotionally vulnerable, frightened, and resentful of certain types of responsibilities. Bethany has no one to help her care for Adam and lacks other activities to keep her life fulfilling and well rounded. A variety of therapies, including counseling, family support, and antidepressant medication, is necessary to help Malcolm and Bethany through this rough period.

It may be easy to understand how interventions like counseling, increased communication between Malcolm and Bethany, and increased help from Bethany's family eases the stress that the couple has been under. But if their marriage and parental difficulties are based mostly in stress and relationship difficulties, how can a medication help Bethany to feel better?

The mind and body work together in complicated ways, and psychological conditions can produce physical changes that warrant medicinal treatment. Sometimes external influences (like relationship difficulties, loss of a job, or financial stress) can have effects on our internal body that can actually change the chemical balance in the brain, causing depression. When the external difficulties are resolved, these chemical imbalances may also resolve, causing the depression to lift. But this is not always the case. In Bethany's situation, Malcolm works to correct the problems he has created for their marriage and to reduce the stress Bethany is under, but Bethany still remains depressed. Even though external conditions have improved, Bethany could still be suffering from an internal chemical imbalance. In this case, an antidepressant or other type of psychiatric medication might help Bethany to get back on a path to mental and physical wellness.

Antidepressants work by adjusting the balance of chemicals in a person's brain. However, finding the correct balance can be difficult, because the chemicals in our bodies are constantly fluctuating in response to numerous environmental, physical, and emotional factors. In the course of a day, you will feel many different sensations and

The fact that antidepressants are usually combined with therapy clouds researchers' ability to accurately measure the effectiveness of antidepressants as a treatment for postpartum and other disorders. If the patient's mood improves after a number of weeks, it may be difficult, or even impossible, to determine whether the improvement is due to the medication, progress in therapy, establishing new support networks, or a combination of these factors.

emotions. You may be angry one moment, frightened the next, and laughing just a little while later. You may feel tired for an hour, but then have a surge of energy. These ups and downs are normal and necessary. Antidepressants do not give a person "happy" chemicals, thereby removing all the downs the person might feel. Rather, antidepressants work to bring the body's own chemicals into a healthy balance so that the person's daily experiences of highs and lows are more moderate. This balance takes time, and an antidepressant medication usually does not have a significant effect on a person's depressive mood for a number of weeks. In the case of postpartum depression, patients and families need to undergo other therapies, such as parenting classes, family counseling, or support groups, in conjunction with drug therapy.

Women with postpartum disorders may experience symptoms ranging from exhaustion and loss of interest in the child, to excessive and debilitating anxiety over the child's health, to delusions and hallucinations. Likewise, there is a great range of psychiatric medications, and different medications can be more or less appropriate for different disorders and symptoms. No drugs have been developed or approved to specifically treat postpartum disorders. Rather, because of the great range of symptoms experienced by mothers with postpartum disorders, different psychiatric medications will be prescribed depending on the particulars of each case. For example, one

A woman's body follows a monthly hormonal cycle that affects her physically and mentally. Childbirth can intensify her hormonal symptoms.

patient with postpartum depression may be given a psychiatric drug for her depressive symptoms, while another patient may only be prescribed a drug to help her sleep. One mother with postpartum psychosis may be prescribed powerful antipsychotic medications, while yet another patient receives no drug treatment at all. There are more than one hundred psychotherapeutic agents listed in the *Physicians' Desk Reference*. Each medical caregiver would use her own discretion to make a selection out of the numerous psychiatric drugs on the market, including antidepressants, antianxiety agents, and antipsychotic drugs.

Selective serotonin reuptake inhibitors (SSRIs) are the most commonly prescribed antidepressants. Having too little serotonin in our bodies can affect our moods, sleep, eating habits, learning, and

Depression: Define it. Defeat it.

Recognizing an emotional problem is often the first step toward healing.

many other important functions. In some people, the cells that produce serotonin begin to reabsorb the serotonin before it can go out and perform its job in the body. SSRIs such as Prozac, Paxil, Zoloft, Celexa, and Luvox keep the cells from reabsorbing the serotonin. Preventing reabsorption allows the serotonin to stay in the body longer, hopefully leading to an increase in serotonin levels and an improvement in the patient's quality of life. The SSRIs are often a good choice for women with postpartum depression because they have a low incidence of anxiety-producing side effects.

A class of psychiatric drugs known as benzodiazepines is also sometimes used when treating women with postpartum disorders. Benzodiazepines such as Ativan, Xanax, Klonopin, and Valium might be prescribed for a woman with anxiety associated with postpartum depression or for the more extreme anxiety that may result from delusions associated with postpartum psychosis. Unlike antidepressants, benzodiazepines work quickly to produce a calming effect, so they can be useful in helping a person in an immediate crisis situation. However, the tranquilizing effect that these drugs have is very powerful and could interfere with a woman's ability to care for her child by affecting her awareness or rendering her unable to respond

Psychiatric medication can help families piece together the emotional "puzzles" that sometimes threaten their happiness.

Brand Names vs. Generic Names

Talking about psychiatric drugs can be confusing, because every drug has at least two names: its "generic name" and the "brand name" that the pharmaceutical company uses to market the drug. Generic names come from the drugs' chemical structures, while brand names are used by drug companies in order to inspire public recognition and loyalty for their products.

Here are the brand names and generic names for some common psychiatric drugs used to treat postpartum disorders:

- Ativan®   lorazepam
- Celexa®   citalopram
- Depakote®   valproate
- Haldol®   haloperidol
- Klonopin®   clonazepam
- Luvox®   fluvoxamine
- Paxil®   paroxetine
- Prozac®   fluoxetine
- Risperdal®   risperidone
- Valium®   diazepam
- Wellbutrin®   bupropion
- Xanax®   alprazolam
- Zoloft®   sertraline

Messages between different parts of the brain are sent using neurotransmitters. If the brain is not communicating properly, it could be the result of an imbalance of neurotransmitters or a malfunction in the parts of the nerve cells that pick up neurotransmitters. In such a case, medications might be helpful in reestablishing the balance of neurotransmitters within the brain or affecting the receptor sites so that they can receive or block certain neurotransmitters. Serotonin is one type of neurotransmitter, and SSRIs affect how this neurotransmitter and its receptors in the brain interact. Changing the way neurotransmitters interact with their receptors can affect emotions. Using medications in this way has been extremely useful in treating some psychiatric illnesses such as depression, anxiety, and bipolar disorder.

to her child's needs. For this reason, such drugs are usually only used to treat mothers in therapeutic settings such as hospitals, where other people will be available to respond to the children's needs. For example, some mothers with extreme cases of postpartum depression or psychosis may become suicidal. If a woman enters the hospital in a suicidal state, benzodiazepines may be used to calm her until she is out of danger of harming herself or her child. Benzodiazepines, however, can also be highly addictive, so once that crisis situation has passed, doctors will begin other approaches for long-term management of the mother's postpartum disorder.

addictive: Having the capability of causing a need for a habit-forming substance.

Like benzodiazepines, beta-blockers are also used in treating anxiety. These drugs block adrenaline, which the body naturally produces in response to stress and anxiety-provoking situations. New mothers are usually under extreme amounts of stress and may have elevated adrenaline levels much of the time. The release of adrenaline causes the heart rate to increase, the muscles to be flooded with blood and oxygen, and energy to surge. If a person is in danger, this flood of energy is vital so the person can protect herself or escape, a reaction known as "fight or flight." In regular life events, however, such as caring for a child, high adrenaline levels can make normal functioning difficult because the brain has turned off thinking and the body has turned on the impulse to fight or run.

A beta-blocker can help a person experiencing things such as obsessive anxiety or hallucinations associated with postpartum psychosis by blocking the adrenaline that is part of the body's immediate fight or flight response. Like benzodiazepines, beta-blockers are not options for long-term treatment of postpartum disorders. However, in some women experiencing dangerous levels of anxiety, the temporary blocking of emotional and physical responses may create valuable openings for therapy to begin.

Dopamine-blocking drugs, such as haloperidol, risperidone, and naltrexone, are used to treat patients with psychotic disorders including schizophrenia. These same drugs are sometimes used to treat women with postpartum psychosis, but it is important to remember that these antipsychotic drugs affect different people's brains in very different ways. In people with psychotic disorders, these drugs can usually be tolerated in large amounts and help to regulate symptoms so patients can lead a more normal life. In people without psychotic disorders, however, very low doses of antipsychotics tend to have a highly sedative effect. Like benzodiazepines, antipsychotic drugs for the treatment of postpartum psychotic episodes should usually be given in hospital or other therapeutic settings where someone will be available to look after the child's needs if the drugs render the mother unable to do so. Relief of symptoms through sedation can be very helpful in extreme crisis situations (like admittance to a psychiatric hospital for a suicide attempt). In such cases, however, other types of drugs or therapies will probably be more appropriate once the crisis period has passed.

A pregnant mother often has high expectations. When reality does not live up to these hopes, she may "crash" emotionally.

Chapter Four

Treatment Description

Elizabeth had never wanted anything more than she had wanted to be a mother. She and her husband had tried for years to have a baby but with no success. Then, six years after they had begun trying, Elizabeth and her husband, Chris, were ecstatic to discover that Elizabeth was pregnant. Five months later, they suffered a devastating blow when Elizabeth had a miscarriage.

After the miscarriage, Elizabeth felt numb. An empty feeling lurked in her mind, but she locked away the feeling. She was afraid that if she acknowledged even one ounce of her sorrow, she would be swallowed up and suffocated, never to resurface again. She regarded her emotions as turbulent water locked precariously behind a leaky dam. If she allowed even one drop to begin trickling through, the whole dam would give way and everyone would drown.

Although attitudes toward women have changed in the twentieth and twenty-first centuries, child raising is still an important part of the role our culture assigns to women.

Elizabeth remained in her protective denial for four months before she finally broke beneath the pressure. Chris tried to coax her out of the depression but was unsuccessful. Thinking that Elizabeth needed help moving beyond their loss, he began talking hopefully about trying again to have a child, but Elizabeth pushed him away in disgust. Filled with remorse but still not understanding what Elizabeth needed, he began looking into adoption and reporting to Elizabeth about the things he learned. Elizabeth refused to listen to his suggestions; she said she never wanted to think about children again. Before long, Chris too began to cave beneath Elizabeth's overwhelming sorrow. He felt completely alone, and he had no idea how to get through to his wife.

Discussion

As we discussed before, the mind and body are connected in very complicated ways. When Elizabeth falls into a deep depression after her miscarriage, the loss of the child is even more difficult for her because she has wanted children for so long and spent so many years trying to conceive. Treatment for Elizabeth's depression would probably focus on therapy to help her through the grieving process.

Postpartum depression, however, is often the result of multiple factors. Although some postpartum disorders might be treated most successfully through psychiatric therapy alone, many cases respond best to a combination of treatments.

Traditional psychotherapy focuses on increasing a patient's awareness of her actions and emotions in an attempt to understand why she behaves and feels a certain way. Psychotherapists believe that once the patient consciously understands her actions and emotions, she will be able to change these actions or resolve the

psychotherapy: An approach to treating mental disorders and emotional problems that focuses on teaching a person to discover, understand, and communicate his internal drives, motivations, and desires.

emotions. In many types of psychiatric conditions, this approach is very successful. In Elizabeth's case, for example, a therapist may be able to help her understand that she is not only grieving the loss of her unborn child but that she is also suffering from the years of disappointment and frustration of not getting pregnant. Further complicating her feelings is the fact that she is immobilized by the fear that further attempts at pregnancy will just lead to more disappointment and sorrow.

Once Elizabeth can clearly identify her emotions, they may seem less overwhelming, and she may feel more prepared to conquer them. In another example, perhaps a mother is suffering from severe anxiety related to postpartum depression that causes her to feel fearful of touching or holding her child. Through psychotherapy, she may tell her therapist about how she was physically abused as a child. She may then realize that the reason she has such high anxiety about caring for her baby is that she is afraid she will hurt her own child in the way her parents hurt her. Once she realizes that her actions are motivated by fear, she can begin working to overcome her fear and behave differently with her baby.

Psychotherapy is a very individual treatment, and each person's treatment plan will be different. The patient should feel both physically and emotionally safe. In the case of postpartum depression, many women suffer from a lack of emotional support as they struggle with their new role as a mother. A therapist's office can be an important place for women to voice their frustrations and feel emotionally supported.

Defining and developing boundaries is another important step in beginning the treatment process. Therapists should also establish guidelines for telephone availability. Most therapists make themselves available by telephone for emergency situations only. Too much reliance on telephone conversation can have an adverse effect on the therapeutic doctor–patient relationship. If a patient calls her therapist every time she feels uncomfortable or confused, she will not learn how to deal with and overcome difficulties on her own. In the case of postpartum disorders, however, therapists and doctors

Drug Approval

Before a drug can be marketed in the United States, it must be officially approved by the Food and Drug Administration (FDA). Today's FDA is the primary consumer protection agency in the United States. Operating under the authority given it by the government, and guided by laws established throughout the twentieth century, the FDA has established a rigorous drug approval process that verifies the safety, effectiveness, and accuracy of labeling for any drug marketed in the United States.

While the United States has the FDA for the approval and regulation of drugs and medical devices, Canada has a similar organization called the Therapeutic Product Directorate (TPD). The TPD is a division of Health Canada, the Canadian government department of health. The TPD regulates drugs, medical devices, disinfectants, and sanitizers with disinfectant claims. Some of the things that the TPD monitors are quality, effectiveness, and safety. Just as the FDA must approve new drugs in the United States, the TPD must approve new drugs in Canada before those drugs can enter the market.

must keep the newborn's well-being in mind as well as the mother's. This may require that therapists or doctors become more involved in cases where limiting a woman's access to medical or psychiatric attention could put the child in danger.

Treatment scheduling is also an important part of therapy, and frequent visits, especially in the early stages of the postpartum period, can be very helpful for women experiencing postpartum depression. In other types of psychiatric illness, therapists may seek to limit contact between themselves and their patients. However, many women suffer postpartum depression in large part because

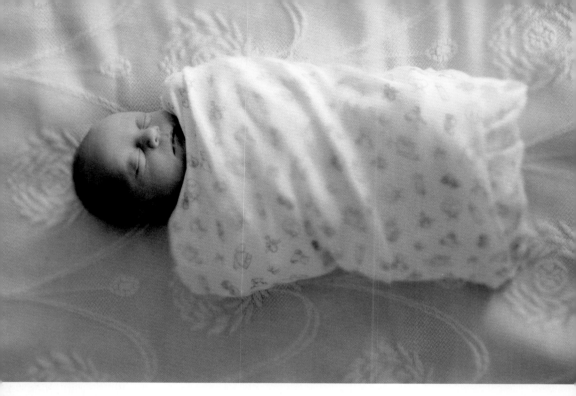

A new baby is a very small bundle that comes with very large responsibilites.

they have been sent home from the hospital abruptly and are ill prepared for the new challenges before them. Even short, frequent visits with a primary care physician can go a long way toward allaying a mother's fears and easing the transition into her new role. However, it is also important that the new mother not become too dependent on a medical professional; she needs to feel that she herself is capable of caring for her child. The patient will eventually move beyond therapy, and when this happens she must know that she can maintain good mental health on her own without her therapist's help.

Therapy for women with postpartum depression is unique in how much it involves members of the family beyond the woman who is feeling depressed. One reason for this is because a mother's postpartum depression not only affects herself but also her new child, her spouse or partner, other children she may have, and other

A mother's depression can also affect the emotional or physical well-being of her child.

As hospital and insurance costs increase, hospital stays for childbirth shorten. Many women in North America are released from the hospital less than forty-eight hours after giving birth. This marks a sudden and often frightening transition for parents—especially for new mothers who have to learn to care for a baby as they go. Some studies suggest that decreased hospital stays and access to medical practitioners leads to an increase in new mothers with postpartum disorders. Hospitals and insurance companies may shorten hospital stays in an attempt to keep down costs, but the treatment of postpartum disorders can add to increased costs in the long run. Improving medical care to give families proper preparation before a postpartum disorder develops is not only beneficial to families but also makes good financial sense.

family members. Furthermore, a woman's depression after childbirth is often related to factors regarding her family's and spouse's involvement in the new child's care. For this reason, therapy frequently includes the woman's relationship partner (if present) or other family members. Including other members of the family through family counseling, parenting classes, the baby's checkups, and so on is often an important aspect in the holistic treatment of postpartum disorders.

Many new mothers are overwhelmed by their responsibilities yet are afraid to ask for help. Asking for help may become confused in some women's minds as admitting to failure. One important part of individual and family counseling may be recognizing that everyone needs help at one time

holistic: Focusing on the whole rather than on parts. Holistic medicine focuses on treating the whole person instead of examining and treating separate parts of the person.

or another and that the need for help does not imply failure. Help, however, is not always as easy to find as one might wish. Concentrating on finding small areas of help each day may be more plausible than finding friends or family who can whisk the children away for a weekend. Some suggestions may include asking for someone to baby-sit while Mom is at home so that she can take a nap, asking a friend or family member to do the grocery shopping or help cook a meal, or finding small tasks that older children can perform to take some pressure off Mom. Support groups in which mothers can gather with other women facing similar challenges can also be immeasurably beneficial in helping to share ideas and break the social isolation that contributes to postpartum depression.

If a patient in consultation with her doctor decides that medication might be a helpful addition to her psychiatric therapy, or might be the most appropriate choice for her primary therapy, she will have to follow the treatment program carefully. In the case of postpartum depression, the doctor would probably begin by prescribing an SSRI. There are a number of different SSRIs, and it would be up to the doctor to decide which of these medications to prescribe. Doctors usually begin by prescribing the medication that has the lowest rate of side effects. However, not every drug works for every person, so a patient may need to try a number of different drugs before finding the one that is right for her. Although some people feel relief within two or three weeks, it can take eight to ten weeks for psychiatric medications to begin taking effect.

Many psychiatric drugs require a weaning-on period—a period of time when the patient takes a smaller than average dose so that her body can get used to the medication. This may affect the amount of time it takes for the patient to experience any benefit from the drug. For example, the typical therapeutic dose for the SSRI Zoloft is 50 milligrams once each day. However, a patient who is just beginning to take Zoloft would

therapeutic dose: The amount of medication that provides a positive effect for the patient.

generally begin by taking a 25-milligram dose once each day so that her body can adjust to the medication. After one week, the dosage should be increased to 50 milligrams once each day. For some people, 50 milligrams of Zoloft is still too little to produce a therapeutic effect. In this case, the doctor would slowly increase the dosage to a maximum of 200 milligrams per day. The amount of time it takes for a patient's body to adjust to a therapeutic dose will affect how long it is before the patient notices any benefits of taking the medication.

metabolized: To be changed within the body.

Some psychiatric medications, such as Depakote, are metabolized by the liver, and patients need to be monitored to protect against liver damage. When beginning a medication like this, the doctor will require routine blood tests to measure how well the patient's body is metabolizing the drug. At first, the doctor may require blood tests as often as every two weeks and will gradually extend the testing period to once every one to three months. For some patients, the medication may help their psychiatric disorder but may begin to damage the liver or other parts of the body. In such a case, the doctor and patient must decide which

Off-Label Prescriptions

The FDA bases its approval on specific research results. Sometimes, a particular use for a drug may have been thoroughly researched by many studies, while other uses lack the same amount of research. In that case, the drug label will only include the uses that have met the FDA's stringent research requirements. Physicians, however, may continue to prescribe that drug for other "off-label" uses.

Regular blood tests are important when taking some psychiatric drugs to monitor the risk of liver damage.

Medication can help a woman cope better with postpartum depression—but it does not provide the entire answer to her difficulty.

presents a more immediate threat, the psychiatric disorder or the medication. In almost all cases in which a medication is threatening liver health or function, the patient must stop taking the medication and look for other medications to help her disorder. However, there can be great dangers in ceasing medications suddenly. Just as many psychiatric medications have a weaning-on period, many also have a weaning-off period during which the patient gradually reduces her daily dosage, allowing her body to adjust before ending the medication completely.

It is important to remember that treating the symptoms of postpartum depression is not always the same as treating the cause of postpartum depression. For example, if Elizabeth's doctor prescribed an antidepressant medication but never tried talking with Elizabeth about why she was depressed, the medication would have a limited and perhaps nonexistent beneficial effect on her condition. To truly help Elizabeth's long-term emotional health, the source of her depression needs to be identified and treated. Sometimes, however, treating the symptoms of postpartum depression with medications can make it easier for a patient to undergo therapy. For example, if Elizabeth is so depressed that she cannot get herself to leave her bed, she will not be able to get herself to the therapy that could help her. If she can bring her depression under control with medication, she may be able to focus on her therapy and make greater strides in overcoming her long-term postpartum depression.

Whether or not a woman decides to use medication as part of treatment, postpartum depression usually resolves within one year of giving birth. When properly treated, postpartum psychosis usually begins to improve within two to three months. However, some women who experience postpartum depression and psychosis may have relapses in the future. At these times, they may have to return to medication or other therapies. Some women with major depression may even find that medications are a necessity in the ongoing maintenance of good health. Many people—not just those with psychiatric conditions—live and thrive because of the help of medication. People with conditions like severe asthma and diabetes must always take medication to maintain good health. Long-term medication for psychiatric conditions can be thought of in the same way.

relapses:
Recurrences of a condition.

Each mother's experience is different.

Chapter Five

Two Women's Stories

Each woman who experiences a postpartum disorder is different; her experience will not be exactly like any other woman's. However, women who suffer from one of these disorders share many things in common. Their stories illustrate the challenges of this disorder—and the hope that is offered by drug treatment and other therapies.

Marie Osmond's Story

In her book, *Behind the Smile: My Journey Out of Postpartum Depression*, singer, actress, and television host Marie Osmond reveals her battle with postpartum depression. She begins her book with a story.

A crying baby can be an enormous source of tension in a mother's life.

I'm collapsed in a pile of shoes on my closet floor. Around and above me hangs my clothing, which is all I can see as I lean against the back wall of the closet. I can see straight up one of my skirts on a hanger right over my head. It looks like a long, dark tunnel with the exit sealed off. It looks like my life right now.

The skirt goes with one of my favorite suits. I've worn it to several happy occasions. I can recall the events, but I have no memory of what it feels like to be happy.

I sit with my knees pulled up to my chest. I barely move. It's not that I want to be still. I am numb. I can tell I'm crying, but it's not like tears I've shed before. My eyes feel as though they have moved deep into the back of my head. There is only hollow space in front of them. Dark, hollow space. I am as empty as the clothing hanging above me. Despite my outward appearance, I feel like a lifeless form.

I can hear the breathing of my sleeping newborn son in his bassinet next to the bed. My ten-year-old daughter, Rachael, opens the bedroom door and whispers, "Mom?" into the room, trying not to wake the baby. Not seeing me, she leaves. She doesn't even consider looking in the closet on the floor. Her mother would never be there.

She's right. This person sitting on the closet floor is nothing like her mother. I can't believe I'm here myself. I'm convinced that I'm losing my mind. This is not me.

I feel like I'm playing hide-and-seek from my own life, except that I just want to hide and never be found. I want to escape my body. I don't recognize it anymore. I have lost any resemblance to my former self. I can't laugh, enjoy food, sleep, concentrate on work, or even carry on a conversation. I don't know how to go on feeling like this: the emptiness, the endless loneliness. Who am I? I can't go on.

In this passage, Marie Osmond gives an articulate and heart-breakingly accurate description of what many women with postpar-

tum depression feel but are never able to express. Her book, however, does more than describe what postpartum depression feels
like. In its honest pages, Osmond explores the many life circumstances, not just the birth of her seventh child, that influenced and
ultimately culminated in her experience of postpartum depression.
She explains,

My postpartum depression was "sensational" for me because I
sensed it in every area of my life. It wasn't "overnight," however.

Today's mothers often juggle many responsibilities.

The normal hormonal changes I experienced, as most women do, after giving birth tipped the apple cart for me, but the depression that resulted had been in the making for years. My PPD wasn't the result of a one-time physical imbalance. Once the debilitating physical symptoms of it were under control . . . to fully recover I found I had to look at my complete state of being, not just physical, but every aspect.

Like Osmond, many women find that their postpartum disorder is caused by multiple factors and that addressing one of those factors (such as treating emotional upheavals with antidepressants) may provide short-term relief. In the long run, however, many women find that treating one symptom is only a temporary fix and eventually the unaddressed aspects of their disorders will lead to a relapse. In such cases, patients may find that they are worse off after a relapse than they were before beginning treatment and feel frustrated and exhausted by the idea of beginning all over again. Because of reasons like these, an approach to treatment that addresses many different aspects of the woman's life is a good place to start from the very beginning.

Marie Osmond describes her recovery from postpartum disorder as consisting of four parts: physical, social, mental, and spiritual. In the first stage of her treatment, Osmond, with the help of a trusted doctor, focused on the physical side of her disorder using hormone replacements, herbal and vitamin supplements, improved nutrition, exercise, and increased sleep to regain her physical health.

Once Osmond felt physically well and strong enough, she began tackling the second stage of her treatment, focusing on the social influences that were contributing to her depression. In this time, she focused on learning to communicate more effectively with her family, allowing herself to share her feelings and ask for much needed help in balancing her multiple roles of mother, wife, and career woman. She cites building her social support network as a key element in her recovery.

In her journey to wellness, Osmond also focused on the mental (or psychological) aspects of her condition. For Marie Osmond, as for

Religion can offer a source of emotional and psychological strength.

so many women, the unacknowledged hurts of the past reared their ugly heads in her depression, blocking her from moving into a happier future. In therapeutic counseling, Osmond found the strength to address long-buried and unresolved issues of abuse in her past. Through counseling, she was also able to rebuild her relationship with her husband—a vital part of her mental, emotional, and social support system.

The fourth, and for Osmond the most important, aspect of her treatment was spiritual. Marie Osmond believes that even if all other needs are met—physical, social, and mental—something is still missing if one is not spiritually fulfilled. Relying on her faith, Osmond found strength to overcome her fears of failure and release her need for constant control. She found, as many people do, that this ability to release the worries that she could not control or change over to a higher power provided tremendous relief and a foundation for all of her other work toward wellness.

It may be strange to think of religion playing a part in a person's medical treatment, but it can be a very powerful thing. Throughout human history, religion has been one of the biggest influences on the development of societies, cultures, and belief systems. As with all societies, religion has had a strong influence on North American society and beliefs. The values of Western religions, such as Judaism, Protestantism, Catholicism, and Islam, influence everything from the way we treat each other to the way we run our governments. Many people in our society are raised within a specific religious belief system, and this belief system will influence how they interpret the events and world around them. Many other people, even if not raised within a religion, turn to religion in times of need, such as when diagnosed with a serious illness. Religion has always been a powerful force in Marie Osmond's life, and in her battle with postpartum depression, religion became a place where she could turn for strength, comfort, and healing.

Michele G. Remington's Story

By the time anyone realized how serious Michele Remington's postpartum disorder was, it was already too late. The bullet meant to kill her had passed mere millimeters from her heart, and Michele's infant son was already dead.

Throughout the 1980s and 1990s, a number of cases in which women suffering from severe postpartum disorders injured or killed their children seized the hearts and minds of North Americans and the appetites of the media. Michele Remington was one of these cases. Many of these stories have helped to increase public awareness, understanding, and support for mothers struggling with postpartum disorders. On the other hand, many of these cases have raised public disbelief and outrage toward the women involved—a sign of how far we still are from truly understanding and knowing how to deal with postpartum disorders.

In the book *The Cradle Will Fall*, Michele Remington and her psychiatrist, Dr. Carl S. Burak, describe Michele's heartbreaking descent into madness and her desperate struggle toward recovery. At the age of twenty-nine, Michele was thrilled to be pregnant. She was one of five children, had always loved and interacted well with kids, and looked forward to having a family of her own. In her past, Michele had suffered brief but intense periods of depression associated with premenstrual syndrome. Later, and once it was too late, psychiatrists would realize that Michele sometimes entertained suicidal thoughts during her monthly bouts with depression and that her premenstrual syndrome could have warned of things to come. But there is no way to determine for certain who will and will not experience postpartum disorders, and hindsight is always twenty-twenty. As it was, Michele's concerns about premenstrual depression faded as her excitement grew regarding her pregnancy and coming child.

As happens with a few women, Michele's experience of pregnancy evolved from joy-filled early days, to morning sickness and irritability, and finally to pain and incapacitating physical complications in the final trimester. As the final months of Michele's pregnancy wore on, she felt herself changing, sinking into herself and becoming mentally withdrawn, first from her physical discomfort and then from her confusing emotions.

Physically and emotionally stretched to her limit, the circumstances surrounding Michele's labor and the birth of her son, Joshua, were the final straw for Michele's delicate emotional state. After more than twenty-five hours of distressed labor, Michele's son was delivered with forceps. He was not breathing. As the doctors worked to save the baby, he began to seize and was rushed by helicopter to a distant hospital.

seize: To have a convulsion.

Although motherhood offers great joys, it is also an enormous adjustment.

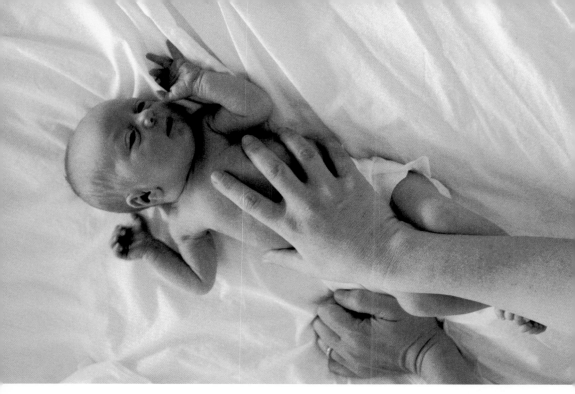

A new baby is completely dependent on others to meet her needs.

Michele never saw her son before he was whisked from the hospital. She was told that his chances of brain damage were high.

Much later, Michele described to her psychiatrist how cheated she had felt in the hours and days after her son's birth. She said that she had gone to the hospital to have a baby, but that baby never appeared. She never saw his face or heard his cry. She felt that she'd been robbed, denied a vital moment in motherhood, the first moment to connect with her son.

Within the first hours of giving birth, Michele was already sinking into a deep depression. Many factors played into her unstable mental state, not the least of which was the fact that one of Michele's brothers was mentally handicapped, most probably as a result of the difficulties experienced during his own birth. Thoughts of her brother and the similarities between his birth and the birth of her son plagued Michele.

It is impossible to know how large a part Michele's inability to see her son at his birth played in her following depression, or even if it played any role at all. However, doctors recognize the extreme importance that the birth process plays in a woman's connection to and relationship with her child. Problems and complications in the delivery of a baby can make many women feel that they have failed as mothers before true motherhood has even begun. Now, even in the most complicated births, most medical personnel try to allow the new mother at least one moment to see her child before additional medical procedures begin.

The same thoughts plagued her other family members as well. In the days and weeks to come, Michele's husband and parents recognized Michele's change of attitude and tried to offer support. In retrospect, they would remark many times that "something was wrong," but as is so often the case, no one knew what to do. Eventually Michele's mother took her to see a doctor, who diagnosed her with postpartum depression. But by that time, Michele was already suicidal. Two days after the appointment, Michele swallowed a bottle of sleeping pills. Two days after this suicide attempt failed, Michele, in the midst of psychotic delusions and hallucinations, shot her son and then herself.

Many people cannot comprehend how a woman could come to kill her own child. In most cases, even the women who commit these acts do not understand their actions or how they came to be. Michele herself, though she has many memories of her suffocating depression, suicidal desires, and hallucinations, does not remember the moment when she picked up the gun and shot herself and her son. Prior to the tragedy, Michele remembers making the decision to shoot herself, but in all the events leading up to that horrible day, she never wished or intended to harm her son.

The aftermath of her son's death was filled not only with Michele and her family's pain but also with the entire community's pain, confusion, and anger. Michele's psychiatric illness quickly became a prevailing focus in the hearts and minds of those who were working in the emergency room on the night of the tragedy, those involved in the pending lawsuit, and people who simply heard of the tragedy through the grapevine of the small community. Many of the nurses, most of whom were mothers themselves, who had worked to save Michele and her son found themselves suffering in the wake of the disaster. They could not reconcile their anger toward Michele with the work they had done to save her life. They felt confused and deeply disturbed, not understanding how a woman—a mother like themselves—could kill her child. In the weeks to come, the experience the hospital staff had with Michele prompted doctors and nurses to reach out to mental health professionals in an attempt to come to terms with their own suffering and learn more about postpartum disorders.

Due to the court's recognition of Michele's postpartum depression and psychosis, Michele was acquitted of criminal charges connected to her son's death. However, hearts and minds do not heal as quickly or efficiently as court decisions are handed down. Michele, her family, friends, and psychiatrist continued to struggle with the ramifications of her postpartum depression, and the tragedy that would haunt them forever.

Despite her still delicate mental and emotional state, Michele eventually decided it was time to speak out about what had happened to her. She knew that other women faced the same psychiatric illness she had faced, and she hoped that her story might make a difference so that these other women would not be overlooked the way Michele had been. Perhaps other women could find help before it was too late.

Michele, along with her husband and psychiatrist, told her story on a now-famous episode of the Phil Donahue show. She cites this experience as the first time she began to feel like "somebody" again.

Telling her story on the Phil Donahue show, and later in the book, became an important part of her recovery. At the end of *The Cradle Will Fall*, Michele states:

> In 1987, my dream of motherhood dissolved in a dark psychotic haze that descended slowly. On a rainy day that seemed most certainly eternal, the life of my baby boy was extinguished forever, my whole self-worth shattered, my personality was shaken apart, and my life was forever altered. I would cause so much heartache and sadness to those who love me, that even now, I cannot find forgiveness for myself.
>
> I can never be the same person I was before that tragic day. I can never undo the chaos and grief I brought to the lives of people who never stopped loving me. I can only hope that this book will help in some way—that some people will be open-minded, willing to take precautions and to gain the knowledge that is so vital. If, through awareness, one life is saved, I will be grateful.

For Michele Remington, treatment for postpartum depression came too late to save her son, but she continues to hope that her story will allow other mothers to be recognized and treated before it is too late for them or for their children. Drug therapy does not hold all the answers for women like Michele—but it may be a place to start.

Medication offers help with postpartum disorder, but all drugs have potential side effects and risks.

Chapter Six

Risks and Side Effects

Nicola looked at the little orange bottle and felt hopelessly torn. She couldn't stand being depressed again. When she first began taking the antidepressant medication, it seemed like it was going to save her life. She felt like she was waking up from being in a three-month coma. The world began to seem right again, like something dark and blurry coming into focus. Everything from three days after the baby's birth to the time she began taking the medication was like one dark and joyless night, but now she was noticing her daughter again and being charmed by all her baby antics. Nicola didn't want to return to that dark place, but she wasn't sure that this medication was the right choice.

When Nicola began taking the antidepressant, her doctor had warned her she might not see any significant effect for a number of

Due to the risk of transferring medications to infants through breast milk, and because postpartum depression usually resolves with time, some women may choose to forego drug treatment and simply "wait out" their depressive symptoms. However, care must still be taken to ensure that the mother–child relationship is not harmed during this period. Maternal–parental coaching emphasizing strategies for playing and interacting with the child can be helpful. Studies have shown that such treatment improves the mother–child relationship and the child's mental and physical development even when the mother's depression remains.

weeks. Nicola thought, however, that her mood began to lift almost immediately. She had discussed the fact that she was breastfeeding her daughter with her doctor, but he said that there was no evidence to suggest this medication could harm her baby. Reassured by her doctor's words, Nicola began the medication and was pleased with the effects.

After two weeks, however, she had begun feeling some side effects. She became nauseated when taking the medication and found that she couldn't eat for two hours after swallowing the pill. This worried her because she tried to eat often in order to maintain enough breast milk for her daughter. The benefits of the medicine, however, seemed to outweigh this slight negative side effect, so Nicola tried to adjust the time of day when she took her medicine so it would have the least impact on eating and breastfeeding.

One month after beginning the medication, however, Nicola noticed a more disturbing side effect. Her daughter had begun having trouble sleeping, accompanied by persistent diarrhea. At first, Nicola was able to attribute her daughter's symptoms to the fussiness and general "messiness" of babies, but now she was sure it was something more. She thought her daughter was also having side effects to the medication. Nicola decided that the best thing to do would be to

The medical and pharmaceutical communities use advertising to encourage individuals with depression to seek treatment.

Psychiatric medications have changed the way we look at depression and other psychiatric disorders, but these drugs can also be dangerous.

continue the medication and switch from breastfeeding to formula. Her doctor supported her choice.

But now she faced a new dilemma. Her daughter hated the formula and the bottle it was presented in. Feeding times had become struggles that often ended with both the baby and Nicola crying. Nicola's attempts to wean her daughter led to heartbreaking, inconsolable tantrums that only breastfeeding seemed to soothe. Her doctor said Nicola had nothing to worry about, that some babies were more difficult to wean than others, and that her daughter would be fine and eventually accept the bottle. Nicola wasn't so sure. She knew that breastfeeding could play an important role in the emotional bond between mother and child. Now, as she tried to coax the confused baby to take the bottle, she felt that she was robbing her daughter of a vital emotional comfort. Her baby's tortured wails made Nicola feel that denying breastfeeding to her daughter might border on emotional abuse. She no longer knew what to do; she thought that her only option might be to stop taking the antidepressant so that her daughter could breastfeed safely again.

Discussion

Everything we put into our bodies has an effect. Most things, we hope, will have a positive effect. Food gives us energy. Water hydrates us. Air provides oxygen to our cells. Unfortunately, other things can have negative effects. Eating peanuts can give energy to one person but can be fatal to a person with a severe peanut allergy. One person may swallow chlorinated water while swimming and feel fine. Another person may swallow the same amount of chlorinated water and feel sick. Medications also have both positive and negative effects. Some people may experience only positive effects of a given medication. For other people, like Nicola and her baby, the negative effects of medication may begin to outweigh the positive gains.

hydrates: Provides moisture to the cells.

When prescribing psychiatric drugs for women with postpartum depression, there are a number of considerations to keep in mind. One consideration is that many women with postpartum depression experience high amounts of anxiety relating to their children's well-being and their own adequacy as parents. A psychiatrist may wish to prescribe an antidepressant for the woman's depressive symptoms, but some antidepressants, like Wellbutrin, can have anxiety-producing side effects. In some cases of postpartum depression with anxiety, the medication that is meant to help the patient could actually make the patient's symptoms worse.

It takes a lot of effort to grow children who are emotionally, physically, and mentally healthy!

With the help of her medical practitioner, each woman must evaluate whether or not medication is the right option for her situation.

Side effects can happen for many different reasons and do not necessarily mean that a person should stop taking her medication. Some side effects are a sign that the dosage of medication is too high—and lowering the dosage might eliminate the side effects while still providing therapeutic benefits. Other side effects may be temporary—something that the patient feels while her body adjusts to the medication, but that will go away with time. Sometimes a patient may even suffer psychosomatic side effects to taking the drug. Side effects like these are caused not by the drug, but by the patient's mind. For example, a patient may read a story about a person who became terribly sick when taking a certain medication. When the doctor prescribes this medication for her, she may be so afraid of getting this illness that her brain actually convinces her body that she is sick, even though the drug did not make her ill. Discussing side

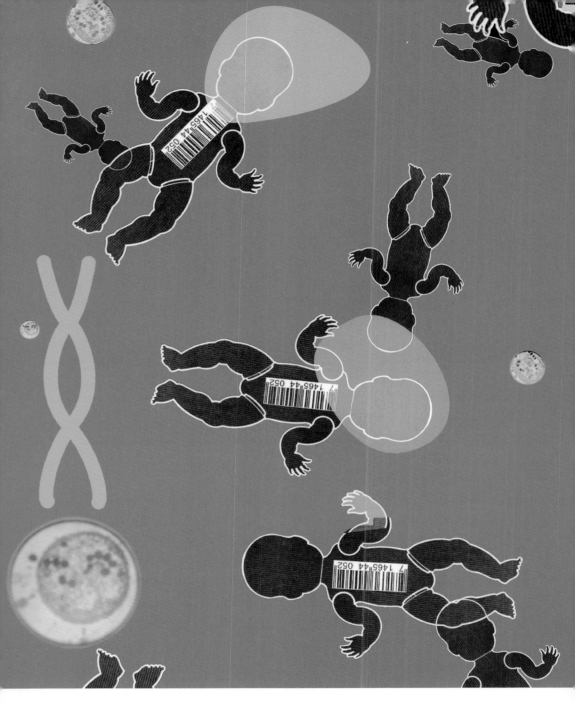

Psychiatric drugs can cause congenital disorders in unborn babies.

effects with a doctor can help a patient to find out what type of side effects she is having and how best to deal with these effects.

Women with postpartum depression must take into account some special considerations when reviewing medications as treatment possibilities. For instance, women planning to take psychiatric medications should consider the effects that these drugs might have on fertility and pregnancy. Some psychiatric drugs affect hormone levels in the body, reducing fertility rates. On the other hand, many psychiatric drugs interact with birth control pills, causing them to lose their effectiveness and increasing the woman's chance of becoming pregnant. A woman with postpartum depression could be devastated to find that she is pregnant again—before she has emotionally recovered from her previous pregnancy. The risk of pregnancy can also be very dangerous, because many of these same drugs can be toxic to the developing fetus. There are cases in which psychiatric drugs have caused congenital conditions such as spina bifida, heart abnormalities, neurological defects, and other birth defects. The vast majority of women taking psychiatric drugs are able to have normal pregnancies and deliver healthy babies, but the benefits and risks of taking medication during pregnancy should always be considered carefully before becoming pregnant.

spina bifida: A birth defect in which some of the spinal column is left exposed.

An additional consideration for women with postpartum disorders is that many drugs can be transferred to a baby through the mother's breast milk, so a new mother who is on psychiatric medications may be unable to breastfeed. Many antidepressant medications, however, do appear to be safe for use while breastfeeding, since they appear to exist only in very low levels in the mother's breast milk. Two specific medications, however, that have been linked to side effects in the nursing baby are fluoxetine and citalopram. Fluoxetine has been associated with crying, disturbed sleep, vomiting, and watery stools in breastfeeding

Some psychiatric medications can affect the balance of women's hormones. However, hormone fluctuations are common in the postpartum period and may contribute to postpartum depression. For this reason, a woman experiencing postpartum depression should have her hormone levels tested and discuss the possible effect psychiatric medications might have on these levels with her doctor. For some women, hormone replacement therapy may be a more appropriate treatment than psychiatric medication.

infants, while citalopram has been associated with disturbed sleep in breastfeeding infants. It is not known whether infants who breastfeed while their mothers are on psychiatric medications face any long-term risks or side effects. The decision to end breastfeeding can be very emotional and difficult on the mother as well as the baby. Many women who decide not to breastfeed or to end breastfeeding early in the postpartum period worry that they are emotionally, physically, or nutritionally denying their children. This is the dilemma that Nicola is facing in her relationship with her young daughter. Discussing concerns about breastfeeding with a doctor, therapist, or with another, more experienced mother can help women with this difficult decision.

somnolence: Sleepiness, drowsiness, or fatigue.

over-the-counter drugs: Medications that are available without a doctor's prescription.

Psychiatric drugs have a great range of side effects. They can cause anything from nausea to sleeplessness to severe neurological dysfunctions like seizures. Some of the most common side effects of SSRIs and mood stabilizers include somnolence, nausea, diarrhea, vomiting, and weight gain. Many psychiatric and other types of drugs cannot be mixed with alcohol, aspirin, over-the-counter drugs, or other medications.

For some psychiatric medications, something as seemingly simple as having a glass of wine with dinner or taking an over-the-counter cold medication could produce serious, even life-threatening effects. Patients must be very careful to discuss these issues with a doctor before they begin taking medication. Many antianxiety drugs can cause chemical dependence. Many mood stabilizers cause fatigue, while many antipsychotic medications induce a tranquilizing effect. The risks and side effects associated with each particular psychiatric drug can be found in The Physicians' Desk Reference.

In some instances, side effects may force a person to stop taking medication, but ceasing medication can also be a complicated process. Suddenly stopping medication can produce negative and dangerous side effects of its own. A doctor can counsel a patient on whether her specific medication can be discontinued immediately or if she needs to taper off slowly.

Although side effects should be taken very seriously, they need not necessarily prevent a new mother from using the psychiatric drugs needed to help her through a difficult time. With her doctor's help, ways to handle side effects can usually be found, allowing the medication to ease her through this difficult time of transition.

Exercise offers opportunities for socialization. Women with postpartum disorders will benefit from both the physical activity and the emotional support to be gained from interacting with others.

Chapter Seven

Alternative and Supplementary Treatments

When Sandra's mother gave her a gift membership to the local gym, Sandra was at first offended. Her mother's poorly veiled hint that perhaps Sandra could stand to lose a few more pounds of that extra baby weight made Sandra feel fat and more depressed than she was already. The first time she dragged herself to the gym she felt more spite toward her mother than gratitude. But when she walked through the doors, everything began to change.

The gym had a clean, well-staffed nursery where her daughter could play while Sandra exercised. Even better, the building was filled with adults her age, all exercising, chatting (in "real" people talk rather than baby talk), playing racquetball, and seeming to have

Regular exercise is one of the best alternative treatments for depression.

a good time. Sandra felt as though she hadn't been in the company of adults for months. She headed for the treadmills and struck up a conversation with the woman working out beside her.

The meeting seemed fated. Barbara was also a young mother, and before Sandra knew what was happening, she was confiding feelings and fears that she didn't know she had. In the time on the treadmill, Sandra told Barbara every aspect of her struggles with being a new mother. She felt embarrassed by how she was expelling her feelings to this total stranger, but Barbara seemed to completely understand. She had a three-year-old and a baby herself and said that she often felt the confusion and depression that Sandra felt. But even more than common experience, Barbara also seemed to have advice and insight for Sandra. She talked about how, after the birth of her first child, she had felt like she was losing control over every aspect of her life. Recovering from an infection following a cesarean section, she was unable to return to work for months. She felt she had lost control over her career, her future, her relationships, even her own body, which now seemed like nothing more than a baby-feeding machine. Sandra exclaimed that she felt the same way and asked what Barbara had done.

Barbara told Sandra that one of the most important steps she had taken in recovering from postpartum depression was reclaiming her body. She described how weak and overweight she felt when her infection finally subsided and that for months she continued on an unhealthy path by sleeping all the time, eating junk foods, and giving in to chocolate cravings. But Barbara realized that much of her own depression was related to feeling she had lost control over her life. Now that she had a baby to take care of, she could no longer control things like when she slept and when she could leave the house, but she realized there were other things she could control, like what she ate and whether or not she exercised. Regaining some control over her body allowed her to feel connected to her independence again. The improvements she saw in her body gave her motivation to tackle other aspects of her life. She requested that her husband take on certain extra responsibilities, like doing the grocery shopping on his way home from work and accompanying her to doctor's appointments. She was even able to begin working part-time out of her home.

More important, however, Barbara told Sandra about the different information and support groups she had found. She said that the Internet had links to numerous resources, such as the organization Postpartum Support International, where she learned about postpartum depression, suggestions and strategies for coping with motherhood, and how to find experienced therapists and support groups in her area. She also told Sandra that the gym had started a new program of therapeutic massage for mothers and

A healthy diet plays a vital role in emotional, physical, and mental health.

Small luxuries—like reading a good book—can contribute to emotional health.

infants that she was going to try and asked if Sandra wanted to join her. Sandra did.

In the next months, Barbara became a close friend and supporter as Sandra worked to turn around her attitude toward motherhood. After meeting Barbara, Sandra decided that she also needed to regain some control in her life. She began choosing to do good things for herself—buying herself small, inexpensive treats, eating healthy and delicious foods, taking time for relaxing baths, and attending the weekly massage sessions with Barbara and their infants.

Eventually, Sandra became an advocate not just for herself but for other women experiencing the hardships that come with new motherhood. Through her friendship with Barbara, she began to realize how many women today feel isolated after giving birth and don't know where to turn for support. This realization led Sandra

A new mother feels a mixture of emotions.

and Barbara to start a mother's group in their town. In the first year, the group consisted of six mothers with a total of nine children. At first the group met once each month to talk about the different challenges the women were facing—and then the group began doing much more. The women got together to do grocery shopping, helped each other clean their houses, took turns baby-sitting so that each mother got time for herself. For the first month after a mother came home from the hospital, the members of the group took turns bringing hot dinners to the mother's home.

Inevitably, there were times when group members couldn't make it to meetings or needed to discuss issues prior to meeting dates, so the women established their own telephone hotline and online forum. Many of the women discussed how they felt that their minds

Being with someone who understands diminishes feelings of loneliness and insecurity.

Marie Osmond discusses humor as an important aspect to her management of postpartum depression and as an important aspect to good mental health in general. She includes the following as symptoms that may indicate a woman is suffering from postpartum disorder:

- Your emotions change so quickly your mood ring explodes on your finger.
- At Halloween, none of the neighborhood kids want to trick-or-treat at the "scary lady's" house.
- Telemarketers hang up on you.
- Your newborn liked you much better from the inside.
- Your baby's first words are, "Take my mother . . . Please!"

were deteriorating as all intellectual pursuits fell to the wayside in the wake of their more immediate responsibilities. To address this issue, the forum became a place for intellectual discussion. Through the forum they discussed issues in the media, started a book club, debated multiple topics, and made contact with other mothers across the continent. In the four years since Sandra and Barbara began the organization, it grew from six to twenty-six mothers, all of whom felt they had become part of a vital support network.

Discussion

As Verta Taylor discusses in her book *Rock-a-by Baby: Feminism, Self-Help, and Postpartum Depression*, the self-help movement has played a major role in many women's ability to recognize and find help for their postpartum depression. In the decades when postpartum disorders were largely ignored by the medical profession, many women found the only place that they could turn was to each other. Now, women's demand for recognition and treatment of postpar-

A new mother's "baby blues" may be intensified if she feels isolated from others.

Psychiatric medication will not turn a mother into "Super Woman"—but it can help her to cope with her life's demands more effectively.

tum disorders has led to many changes in the medical field and more awareness of psychiatric and drug therapies. Nevertheless, self-help and group therapy still play a large role in many women's management of postpartum depression.

Though most doctors might not recommend support groups as the primary source of treatment for a person with a postpartum disorder, these same doctors usually recognize such social networks as vital supplementary therapies to whatever primary care is chosen. New mothers often feel as Sandra did, isolated from other people, particularly from other adults. In support groups, women can meet other mothers who are experiencing the same difficulties, who understand the hardships and guilt associated with a postpartum disorder. New mothers can find other people to relate to who sympathize with their experiences. Because the members of support groups are experiencing similar medical, psychological, and social challenges, patients can be an important resource for each other, sharing information on treatments, doctors, lessons they have learned, and ideas for coping.

As with any treatment method, support groups also have their risks. Some support groups are run by trained professionals; others are not. Some people may use support groups as outlets for frustration and negative feelings, turning what is meant to be positive into a negative experience. There is also the danger of becoming too reliant on the group and losing the ability to cope outside of the support network. As with all treatments, a patient should research carefully before entering into a treatment program.

Many people find help from supplementing their major therapy with smaller therapeutic elements they can incorporate into their daily lives. These smaller elements can be especially important for new mothers whose time is severely limited and who may be unable to attend more time-consuming therapy or support group sessions. For example, doing little things like stopping for a cup of chamomile tea during the day or soaking in a hot bath with lavender-scented oil after work can do a lot to ease day-to-day stress and tension. Taking yoga and meditation classes can teach people valuable relaxation

Even though they are natural remedies, herbs can still have powerful effects on the body and can interact with other medications. Just because a remedy is labeled "natural" or "herbal" does not mean that it is safe, either for the mother taking the remedy or for the breastfeeding child. The U.S. Food and Drug Administration has not approved these substances for medicinal use. For this reason, these substances are not subject to the same rigorous quality controls that apply to approved drugs. Even if the herb itself is safe for ingestion, there is no guarantee that the herb has been manufactured in a pure or safe way. A woman should always discuss the risks of herbal treatments for herself and for her breastfeeding child with a trained physician.

Ginseng is an Asian herbal therapy used to treat depression and tension.

Rhodiola Rosea

Extracts of the plant Rhodiola rosea have only recently appeared in the North American herbal market. However, people as far back as the Vikings have been taking the herb (usually in the form of tea) for its perceived physical and mental benefits. In Russia, soldiers attempting to reduce stress and boost their energy drank tea made from the root of Rhodiola rosea. Today, numerous studies are being conducted on this herb, its possible benefits, and its possible side effects. Researchers now believe that its benefits may be the result of a number of chemical reactions including reduction of the stress hormone cortisol, an increase in hormones that positively affect mood, and a surge in the molecule adenosine triphosphate that cells use for energy.

skills that can be called on in times of stress and crises. New studies have also shown that therapeutic massage has great benefits for both mothers suffering from postpartum disorders and for their infants. Massage can be stress reducing for mothers, while learning the techniques of infant massage can improve emotional bonding between mother and child.

Many drugs can treat the depression of a postpartum disorder, but for some women, medication is not an option. Some women use instead a number of herbal and other natural alternatives. Natural alternatives to medication may include vitamins, dietary supplements, and herbs such as ginseng, dong quai, Saint-John's-wort, kava, and valerian.

Though not approved in the United States for medicinal treatment, ginseng root has been used in Asian medicine for centuries. Supporters of herbal therapy believe ginseng has many beneficial effects—from boosting the immune system to increasing energy levels to aiding in stress management and depressive symptoms.

Natural medications are not regulated by the FDA.

Ginseng is widely available in numerous forms, including teas, pill, and extract form. However, thorough research should be done before beginning this or any other herbal remedy.

Dong quai is another herb that has been used for centuries in Chinese and other medicines. It is thought to positively affect the uterus and hormone balances. Some herbalists recommend dong quai supplements in the puerperium and postpartum periods when a woman's body is recovering from childbirth.

Saint-John's-wort has been used for many centuries for treating both physical and mental illnesses. This herb has been used in Greece, China, Europe, and North America. Studies in Europe have found Saint-John's-wort to be very effective in treating depression and anxiety, but the U.S. Food and Drug Administration has not approved it for such treatments. Though it can be purchased over the counter in health food, grocery, and drugstores, one should still do careful research before beginning any medicinal regimen.

Kava, like Saint-John's-wort, is another herb that has been used to treat depression and anxiety. Kava is a member of the pepper family and grows in the South Pacific islands. Kava root seems to have a calming effect on the mind. It is also used as a muscle relaxant. In European studies, kava root was said to have the beneficial properties of benzodiazepines but without the negative side effects. In very high doses, however, kava may have side effects of its own, including sleepiness and skin irritation. It can be purchased over the counter but has not been approved for medicinal use by the Food and Drug Administration.

Valerian is another herb that has been used for centuries both as a sleep aid and as a temporary remedy for anxiety. It seems to act as a sedative, but as with most herbal remedies, it is not approved by the Food and Drug Administration for medicinal use.

Other herbal remedies exist for conditions such as depression and anxiety. You can find more information on them at your local library or online. Many women, however, are able to obtain relief by making simple but significant lifestyle changes. A person has many options before resorting to drugs and complicated herbal remedies.

If depression, anxiety, and other difficulties plague you, look at your lifestyle first. Do you get a proper amount of sleep? Do you get that sleep at appropriate times (from 10 p.m. to 6 a.m. versus 3 a.m. to 1 p.m.)? Do you eat a healthy diet rich in fruits and vegetables and low in fats and sugars? Do you exercise regularly and spend some time outdoors every day? Sometimes, the smallest first steps are the most important ones in changing our lives.

Further Reading

Bennett, Shoshana and Pec Indman. *Beyond the Blues*. San Jose, Calif.: Moodswings Press, 2011.

Kendall-Tackett, Kathleen H., and Phyllis Klaus. *The Hidden Feelings of Motherhood: Coping with Stress, Depression, and Burnout*. Amarillo, Tex.: Pharmasoft Publishing, 2005.

Kleiman, Karen. *The Postpartum Husband*. New York: Xlibris, 2001.

Osmond, Marie, with Marcia Wilkie and Dr. Judith Moore. *Behind the Smile: My Journey Out of Postpartum Depression*. New York: Warner, 2001.

Resnick, Susan Kushner. *Sleepless Days: One Woman's Journey Through Postpartum Depression*. New York: St. Martin's Press, 2000.

For More Information

The Center for Postpartum Health
www.postpartumhealth.com

The Online PPD Support Group
www.ppdsupportpage.com

The Postpartum Stress Center
www.postpartumstress.com

Postpartum Support International (PSI)
www.postpartum.net

The Mayo Clinic
www.mayoclinic.com/health/postpartum-depression/DS00546

Publisher's Note:
The websites listed on this page were active at the time of publication. The publisher is not responsible for websites that have changed their address or discontinued operation since the date of publication. The publisher will review and update the websites upon each reprint.

Index

About the Author & Consultants

Autumn Libal is a graduate of Smith College and the author of many educational books. She lives and works in Canada.

Mary Ann McDonnell, Ph.D., R.N., is the owner of South Shore Psychiatric Services, where she provides psychiatric services to children and adolescents. She has worked as a psychiatric nurse at Franciscan Hospital for Children and has been a clinical instructor for Northeastern University and Boston College advanced-practice nursing students. She was also the director of clinical trials in the pediatric psychopharmacology research unit at Massachusetts General Hospital. Her areas of expertise are bipolar disorder in children and adolescents, ADHD, and depression.

Donald Esherick has worked in regulatory affairs at Rhone-Poulenc Rorer, Wyeth Pharmaceuticals, Pfizer, and Pharmalink Consulting. He specializes in the chemistry section (manufacture and testing) of investigational and marketed drugs.